Valérie Tasso was born in France and lives in Spain. She has worked at a senior level in corporate PR, and is now an actress and journalist. Her story first appeared in Isabel Pisano's European bestseller about the hidden lives of prostitutes (*Yo, Puta*).

INSATIABLE

The Sexual Adventures of a French Girl in Spain

Valérie Tasso
Translated from the Spanish by Nick Caistor

CORGI BOOKS

INSATIABLE
A CORGI BOOK : 0 552 77272 0

Originally published as *Diarió de una Ninfomana* by
Plaza y Janés, Random House Mondadori in 2003.

First publication in Great Britain

PRINTING HISTORY
Corgi edition published 2005

1 3 5 7 9 10 8 6 4 2

This is a true story. The characters are authentic, the events
are real. But the names and identifying details of certain
individuals have been disguised in order to protect
their anonymity.

Set in 11/14pt Palatino by
Falcon Oast Graphic Art Ltd.

Corgi Books are published by Transworld Publishers,
61–63 Uxbridge Road, London W5 5SA,
a division of The Random House Group Ltd,
in Australia by Random House Australia (Pty) Ltd,
20 Alfred Street, Milsons Point, Sydney, NSW 2061, Australia,
in New Zealand by Random House New Zealand Ltd,
18 Poland Road, Glenfield, Auckland 10, New Zealand
and in South Africa by Random House (Pty) Ltd, Isle of Houghton,
Corner Boundary Road & Carse O'Gowrie, Houghton 2198, South Africa.

Printed and bound in Great Britain by
Cox & Wyman Ltd, Reading, Berkshire.

Papers used by Transworld Publishers are natural, recyclable
products made from wood grown in sustainable forests. The
manufacturing processes conform to the environmental
regulations of the country of origin.

INSATIABLE

My 1,200-Metre Marathon

Encounters may be brief, but no two are ever the same . . .

I lost my virginity on 17th July 1984, at 02.46.50 in the morning. When you're fifteen, you never forget a moment like that.

It happened when I was on holiday at the house of my friend Emma's grandmother, in a mountain village in France.

I immediately fell in love with the place and its smell of eternity, and with the group of boys we went around with. But only one of them really caught my eye: Edouard.

The grandmother's house had a beautiful garden and was right next to a stream that brought a cool breeze to the summer heat. Opposite the house was a field full of grass at least a metre tall, typical of somewhere where it rains a lot. Emma and I spent whole afternoons hidden there, lying on our backs chatting about the boys, and flattening the grass with our heavy, pubescent bodies. At night, we would climb over the garden wall to meet up with the boys again and flirt.

I never told Emma what had happened. One night, Edouard took me to his place. I remember I didn't feel a thing, apart from a sense of shame that I had not bled at all, as well as the strange sensation that I had wet the bed. I left his house under cover of the noise of the lavatory chain, which I pulled to hide the sound of my footsteps on the stairs.

Eleven years later I saw Edouard again, at a conference organized in a Paris hotel. We locked ourselves in the men's bathroom, trying to rediscover the impulse we had felt more than a decade earlier, either from a fear of growing up, or simple nostalgia. But it wasn't the same, and once again the sound of a flushing toilet heralded my disappearance – this time for ever – from his life.

After that first time, I began to feel guilty, and tried to overcome or at least mitigate my feelings of guilt by repeating the experience as often as I could until I reached adulthood. It was not so much that I had abnormally precocious desires, more that I wanted to experiment, out of a sense of pure curiosity.

At first, I put these impulses down to the fact that Mother Nature had endowed me with a special sensibility, which I responded to through my body. This lasted until I enrolled at university at the end of the Eighties.

While I was studying, I was more concerned with my career than with boys. I wanted to be a diplomat, but in the end I changed to Business Administration and Applied Foreign Languages, and graduated without much effort.

My family had taught me good manners, the art of behaving properly, and this, combined with a fairly traditional education and difficulties in communicating, meant I increasingly kept my feelings to myself. A well-brought-up girl like me could never tell her parents she had started her love life so soon.

My sexual life reawakened in my last year at university. I realized I had something special about me which attracted men. I was a witch, and set about discovering enchanting Merlins all over the city: men with some spark to them, lovers, especially those whose veins I could see beneath the skin: I thought that was really sexy. Men whose pulse I could feel at their wrists. Men who could hear a pen scraping on paper, who got emotional at the size of an ink blot on a white sheet of paper. Men who like me could see the particles that made up the air around us, who could see its different colours. People for whom the smell of a blocked toilet in a discotheque at four in the morning made them reflect on the fragility of human existence.

People who made me feel alive.

I know deep down that this search of mine was the symptom of a terrible sickness: silence, solitude, lack of communication. That's why I decided to write down my experiences in a diary. That was the only way I had to explain myself and communicate. I had already tried the most natural way, that is by talking, but I was always very clumsy, because the words came out without me being able to control them. I found it impossible to state my ideas, which was no way for a diplomat to embark on her career.

My real communication began with my body, the

sway of my hips, the way I looked at people. Whenever I got a 'yes' for moistening my lips with my tongue, or for a gaze at someone, or a 'no' for holding my hands across my lap, I began to understand.

Some men like women to talk while they're making love. I've never been able to do that properly, and it's brought me many disappointments. Several men vanished after our first date, even though they admitted I was a good lover; according to them, they needed more communication.

'What do you know about communication?' I would retort, pushing them out and slamming the door in their face.

I began to realize that people needed to put a name to things, to simplify them by using words. This gave them the mistaken impression they were understanding them. I, on the other hand, started to communicate less and less through words, and increasingly with my body.

If you want to define me with a word, go right ahead, I couldn't care less. But you should know that in reality I am a nymph. A Nereid, a dryad. A nymph, nothing more.

The Aphrodisiacal Power of Coca-Cola

20th March 1997

Today I got a call at the office from Hassan. Hassan! It's two years since I last heard from him.

'Traitor,' was the first thing he said. 'You vanished. But as you see, I know where to find you. I have to go to Barcelona this week for my newspaper. I'd like to see you.' Hassan . . .

For two years (not continuously) I had an affair with Hassan. He had (perhaps still has) a special obsession with pushing empty Coca-Cola bottles up my vagina. First he made me drink them, then . . . I've no idea where his obsession with Coca-Cola, or rather the bottle, comes from. I suppose he must have a complex about his penis – and, truth to tell, it doesn't exactly have much artistic or physical prowess.

Apart from sex, we didn't talk much, but we shared a love of Saint-Exupéry's *The Little Prince*, and we both dreamt about what a real love story should be like,

11

sighing deeply. But I always knew he was not my love story. He is Moroccan, I am French. And in some way or other I knew he wanted me as his lover so that he could fuck the whole of France and colonialism.

So today there was no sex, simply a phone call and interesting possibilities . . .

22nd March 1997

Today as I was leaving home I saw a guy in the street. Just by exchanging glances, we decided to make love. As soon as we got into a hotel on the Via Augusta, he took me in his arms and led me to the kitchen, where he laid me on the marble worktop as gently as though I were a china doll. At first, he scarcely dared touch me. But then he pulled off my sweat-drenched tee shirt and held it to his face. All at once he started taking deep breaths and sniffing at the shirt, centimetre by centimetre. He was breathing its sweaty smell in as hard as he could. I could not help staring at him, delighted by his fetishism that was new to me. Beads of sweat stood out like pearls on his forehead, and trickled down between his eyebrows. I leaned over him and started delicately licking them, drinking him in. I could feel his uneven panting right next to my cheek. Excitement gripped my stomach; my thighs twitched. I was losing control. I began to feel giddy, as my body cried out to be stripped bare, to become one with this stranger. He bent towards me, and felt under my skirt until his fingers touched the elastic on my panties. I thought he was going to take them off, but no: instead he raised my skirt and pushed them aside. And took me there and then, his eyes still fixed on mine, searching for every reaction my face showed, every expression.

When we said goodbye in the street, I had no wish to ask him for his phone number. And he had no intention of giving it me. I'm not in the habit of spoiling a meeting like that with a promise to see someone again. A repeat session with a stranger doesn't interest me. I prefer to pick up someone else in the street.

23rd March 1997

Today Hassan arrived in Barcelona. We agreed to meet at the Majestic Hotel.

'Come at seven. Ask for the key in reception and go straight up to the room. I'll be there a bit later. Please be discreet. I'll be coming with my bodyguards. You know the score . . .' he told me on the phone this morning.

I arrived at the hotel five minutes before the agreed time. I asked for the key and got into the elevator. Some fat foreign businessmen made me squeeze into a corner and almost crushed me. Just thinking about all that flesh oozing cholesterol made me feel nauseous. I'm sure none of them has an exactly full sexual life. And besides, their sort always leave you wet with perspiration, because they sweat like pigs.

When we reached the right floor I got out of the elevator. I could feel the swine examining every centimetre of my body from the waist down, with particular emphasis on my backside. If they carry on like that, I thought, I'll haul them all off to my room, even though I've got something much better to do.

I opened the door to the room, drew back the curtains

to let a bit of natural light in, and then headed straight for the minibar, with the firm intention of removing all the Coca-Cola bottles. I wasn't in the mood for any sadomasochism, however *light*. I was quite happy though to perform my best striptease for Hassan, a belly dance without the veils.

I always get nervous before one of these encounters. I switched the TV on and started zapping channels to the rhythm of my heartbeat. Eventually I fell asleep. The sound of the door opening woke me. It was him.

'Why aren't you undressed yet?' he asked reproachfully.

So much for my planned striptease. He made love to me silently with a passion he had never shown before, right there on the carpet. We changed positions several times as if we wanted to share the uncomfortable floor, and the scratchy carpet fibres. I suddenly imagined all the millions of mites we must be squashing; just thinking of them made me sneeze uncontrollably for minutes on end. Hassan took me out of this microscopic zoo by licking me all over. I was surprised at the time he took to see me get pleasure, without thinking of himself. It was his way of rediscovering me after such a long time, with no need to speak. It occurred to me that like good wine, some people improve with the years.

'You remind me of an actress I once had a relationship with,' he said, stroking my hair after soaking my stomach with his semen. 'She always used to tell me: "You can't imagine how many kilometres of dicks I've sucked just to be famous!"'

He burst out laughing.

'A Moroccan actress?'

14

He nodded, and drew deeply on the cigarette he had just lit. Then he put it between my lips. Though I've never liked the taste of a damp filter tip, I accepted it all the same.

'That's some confession! I could understand it in Europe, but in Morocco? Anyway, what's that got to do with me?' I asked, half seriously, leaning up on my left elbow.

'Nothing. Just that you remind me of her. I don't know why, but I saw her face in my mind.'

After an impromptu fellatio, I calculated that if a man's prick measures an average of twelve centimetres, in order to get beyond a kilometre and reach a miserable 1,200 metres, I would have to fuck ten thousand men. Or do it ten thousand times with the same man. I don't think much of that second option. Much more interesting to go for the ten thousand. I'll stick with that hypothesis.

'Fuck that friend of yours, Hassan!'

'What's wrong with her?' he wanted to know, lying there with his legs still spread wide and cupping his balls in his hand.

I shrugged and got up to go to the bathroom. I felt sticky, and wanted to wipe off the semen I had all over my body with some toilet roll, and then have a shower.

I did not want to spend the night with Hassan. I needed to get up early, go home and change my clothes because I had an important meeting to attend. As soon as my lover fell asleep, I left without a sound. I always leave like a cat.

Ten thousand men. I must see how far I've got some day.

25th March 1997

'Will you come to Madrid with me?' Hassan asked. 'I can't miss the event at the Zarzuela Palace. And I'd like you to help me to translate what the papers say about the meeting.'

Not entirely convinced, I decided to go with him. I reserved a room in the Miguel Angel Hotel, and we took the last evening flight. In mid-air, while he was absorbed in his newspaper, Hassan started openly to stroke my legs. I could see the people next to us becoming uncomfortable, so I opened my legs a little wider, for Hassan to be able to run his hand right up the inside of my thigh. Our neighbours looked the other way in disgust. Some other passengers tried to glance surreptitiously at us out of the corner of their eye, but I stared at them and they soon looked away. I have always been astonished at how hypocritical people are. They throw their hands up in horror, yet at the same time they have a morbid fascination for what others are doing.

When we got to the hotel, Hassan suggested we make love in the shower. I was delighted with the idea. When we were both standing in the tub, with the water coursing down my back and his legs, he took the bar of soap and started rubbing it against my pubic hair. Then he reached up and started to soap my nipples. He began to play with them, his hand circling round and round. The slippery sensation of the water and the soapy foam had an immediate effect on my body. Hassan's movements got more and more rapid, so I felt backwards and guided his penis into its natural habitat. Five minutes later, we both came at the same time.

26th March 1997

While Hassan was at his meeting with the heir to the Spanish throne, I tried to link up with Victor López, who works in offices not far from my hotel. Victor and I had met in the Dominican Republic, where every weekend we made love for everyone to see on the Playa Bavaro. During the week, I was in Santo Domingo, and he worked in Santiago de los Caballeros. Four hundred kilometres apart. I wanted to see him again, because I was getting bored cooped up in my room.

'Who shall I say is calling?' his secretary said, icily. I suspect that like many women, she's in love with her boss and doesn't like the idea of putting through a call from another woman. Especially if she sounds attractive.

'A friend of Victor's,' I replied, trying to sweeten her a bit.

'He's not available at the moment. But if you leave me your number, I'll get him to call you as soon as he's free.'

If you don't give him my message I'll kill you, I thought to myself.

An hour later, Victor rang.

'I can't believe it! What part of the world are you ringing from?' he asked, sounding overjoyed to hear from me.

'Well, I gave your secretary my mobile number to throw her off the scent, but in fact I'm very close by, Victor.' My mysterious tone intrigued him.

'You are?'

I could tell from his voice he wanted to see me at once.

'Go on, tell me where you are!'

'I'm in Madrid. I'm staying at the Miguel Angel. But

I'm with someone. So I could have a quick coffee with you, but nothing more.'

'No, don't say that! I need to have dinner with you at least. You're always appearing and disappearing. When am I going to get more than an hour with you?'

He sounded really upset.

'I could have dinner with you perhaps, but that depends on whether or not the person I'm with has a business engagement tonight. Let's have a coffee first and then see what happens, OK?'

I hung up, then rushed to the bathroom to freshen up a bit. I took a jacket from the wardrobe and suddenly decided to light a cigarette. While I was sitting on the sofa smoking – I had to be patient, because I hate arriving first – I started imagining Victor's prick. What did it smell of? How did Victor like to make love? I thought back to our encounters. Got it! He usually preferred the missionary position. Well anyway, I doubted whether I'd get the chance to find out right now.

I finished the cigarette and decided to go downstairs. I had waited long enough. When I reached the lobby, I looked all round to see if he had arrived.

All of a sudden, a hand grabbed me by the waist, and prevented me from turning to see who it was. Then he wrapped his arms round me. We stayed in our passionate embrace for several minutes, despite the looks and giggles of the receptionists, who didn't know where to put themselves. Afterwards, Victor took my chin in his hand, lifted my face, and gave me a kiss on both cheeks.

'I'm so happy to see you! I thought you were in some far-off country, signing contracts. Are you still working for that same firm?'

18

'Yes, but there've been big changes in the group, so I don't know what the future holds. Whatever happens, in the next six months I've got two trips I can't get out of. Next week I have to go to France for a few days to see my grandmother. Then I go to Peru and Mexico. I don't want to get involved in all these internal restructuring problems. I'm off, and we'll see what happens when I get back.'

'What brings you to Madrid? Work?'

'Not really. I came for a few days to accompany a friend, a newspaper editor. He's here to cover a meeting of diplomats.'

I could tell my explanation didn't really convince him.

'There must be something more to it than that. Go on, tell me the truth!'

I carried on explaining.

'Well, what I didn't say was that this gentleman is a friend who has squatter's rights. But that's no surprise to you, is it?'

'That's my Val! Yes! That's what I like . . . Tell me all about it. You're the only person in the world I can talk to about these things without worrying about any taboos or prejudices. What's it like with him?'

I could see I had aroused his curiosity. Deep down Victor had always been rather repressed; someone who could only let himself go when we were together.

'I'm not going to tell you any details. All I'll say is we get on fine, but it could be better.'

'Better? How? Come on, I'll buy you a drink in the bar and you can tell me everything,' he said, obviously angling to hear all about my relationship with Hassan.

But I didn't tell him a thing. I've never liked to boast

about my affairs. Especially when someone like Hassan is involved. You never know. I've told other people about some of the strangers I've met, but never about Hassan.

We said goodbye after two hours, most of which I managed to spend getting him to tell me what was going on in his life.

When I got back to my room, I was surprised to find Hassan already in the bathroom.

'What are you doing here so soon?' I asked him.

Obviously irritated, he replied with another question. 'Where did you get to?'

That night we didn't make love. Hassan said he was tired, but I knew it was his way of punishing me for having given my attention to someone or something other than him.

27th March 1997

Hassan left the hotel early this morning. There was a press conference at Zarzuela Palace, and while he was dressing he went over the questions he had written on a piece of recycled paper. I meanwhile was mentally planning what to do with my day. I had no desire to go shopping or to the Prado museum. In the end, I had four sexual encounters. Two in the morning, two in the afternoon: a perfect balance.

The first was in the metro. With the excuse that the compartment was full, a man touched my backside. We got off at the next station and I greedily set to work on his throbbing prick in an instant-photo booth.

The second was around one o'clock in the afternoon,

after I'd had a bite to eat. I was finishing my roll in Retiro Park, near the Palacio de Cristal, standing behind a tree with squirrels playing all around me – they looked just like hairy, shrivelled human beings – when a man came up and asked if I'd make love with him if he paid me. I refused the money, but agreed to give him pleasure. I couldn't give a damn about money. I'm too curious a person to accept that kind of deal. Besides I reckon I'm priceless. We didn't have much physical contact while we were doing it, because although I warmed to my task, I was always aware of the other people in the park. I didn't want to be taken away by two cops to a police station.

I had agreed to see Victor again later that afternoon. He came straight up to my room. I knew Hassan wouldn't be back till late, so I allowed myself a few hours with an old friend. We talked about the times we had enjoyed in the Dominican Republic, then all of a sudden Victor took me in his arms. Our bodies came together in a lengthy kiss, full of promise for what was to follow. I took off his shirt, revealing his manly chest covered in a dense forest of hair. His skin was red-hot with desire. He removed my blouse and started to stroke my breasts, held in a bra designed to lift and compress the poor little things so they don't look so forlorn. His hands moved round and round. Then he gently laid me back on the bed, holding my head in one hand so I would not bang it against the board. He started kissing my legs with his slightly moist lips, and the silent room was filled with the tiny noises his avid mouth made on my skin. By the time his mouth was licking all round my sex, I could scarcely contain myself. We made love, and came together. We soon wanted more, and this time I took the initiative. I knew he would like what I was doing, and he didn't need much persuasion.

By the time Hassan returned, I was stretched out on the bed watching television. He didn't seem to suspect a thing, but he was in the same bad mood as the previous evening. He told me he had to return to Morocco the next morning, and that we would say goodbye in the airport.

My Encounter With Cristian

28th March 1997

First thing in the morning we were at Barajas airport. Hassan said goodbye in a quick, cold fashion – he doesn't like public displays of emotion. That's the way he is. I have no idea when I'll see him again. I didn't ask him, either. Then I caught the shuttle plane to Barcelona, where I had a heavy day in front of me. In the evening I had a date with a bank manager, to whom I had once given my personal telephone number on my business card. Now he was inviting me to dinner. I never expected him to call me, but he did. So I had to make sure I looked my best.

After work I began the ritual I go through whenever I have a date. I started with a shower, using my Crabtree and Evelyn sandalwood gel, perfect for this kind of occasion. I love the smell, because they say it's an aphrodisiac. Its slightly woody perfume intoxicates me, and I want it to do the same to my skin. I poured it onto my hand, rubbed it all over my feet and legs, then my whole body. While the lotion was drying, I had a quick cigarette. Then I dried myself, and put on the same perfumed body lotion.

As I was putting on my evening clothes – an emerald green dress with see-through stockings and high-heeled shoes – I was thinking of moments like these before a new encounter, when you are so full of expectation and desire. They really are the best. That's why tonight I had no intention of surrendering easily. I wanted the feeling to last. First, I thought, we'll go out to eat. During the meal, I'll arouse him: I'll hand him my panties and stockings as a foretaste of what's to come. I want him to imagine every inch of my body with nothing in the way. I want him to smell my desire. That's what I'll do: I'll hand him my underwear. Then while he's chewing on his peppered steak he can imagine what my sex smells like.

I put on a little make-up, but not too much. I don't want eyeshadow running down my cheeks at our first contact. That's enough to make anyone look like a cheap whore. A little gloss on my lips. Some rouge on my cheeks. A soft white line on the inside of my eyes. That's enough.

The doorbell rang at the agreed time and when I went down I found myself facing a really attractive man. It's strange, but he wasn't how I remembered him. He was wearing a navy blue silk tie with subtle flecks of purple. His classic-cut suit was also navy blue, and his white shirt gave him an irresistibly elegant touch. The shine on his shoes told me he must have just cleaned them, and that he put a lot of effort into whatever he considered important.

Cristian had a smile like a 1950s movie star, with two tiny dimples at the corners of his mouth. The first time I met him I could tell he was a very sensitive sort. He was bound to be a good lover.

And yet last night, absolutely nothing happened between us. Despite the fact that we didn't have much to say to each other, I didn't dare carry out the plan I had dreamt up to fill the silence. There was no stealthy passing of stockings under the table, no titillation from me. But when he asked if he could see me again, I said yes, breaking one of my golden rules.

Night of 29th March 1997

I've come to visit an Italian friend, Franco, and his family, in the countryside. I found it easy to fall asleep, partly because the pure country air exhausted me. I had a strange dream; what most stuck in my memory was the way my image changed. I had dark black hair like a Japanese woman, cut short just above my shoulders with a fringe almost down to my eyes. It was a wig. I was horrified to see myself like that, because it was an image I had been forced to adopt. But it was perfect for the kind of work I had to do. I remember I was in a sort of convent with lots of other girls. At night we would go up to the first floor to work, where there was a geisha house.

I woke up in a sweat, and lit a perfumed candle to help me relax. I breathed in the scent and lay on my back on the bed, with my arms stretched out. I felt as if I were flying through the air. It may sound strange, but I saw my soul rise from my body and fly. All of a sudden I felt someone (a man, I think) grabbing me by the arms and pulling, so that I would take him with me. I was trying to get him off, but I could not move properly. When he realized he could not hold me back, he fell on top of me. He was wearing a dark tunic, and to stop him penetrating me, I switched the light on and lit a cigarette. I had a feeling I was not alone in the room. I was terrified.

My friend Sonia gave me her interpretation of the dream. According to her, the man in the black tunic represented all my phobias and negative energies, and it was a good sign that I had managed to free myself from him.

'It's the announcement of a new stage in your life,' she told me, proud to be a clairvoyant for a day.

30th March 1997

At last I've come to France for a few days with my beloved granny. When she finally released me from all her hugs and sloppy kisses on both cheeks, I went up to the bedroom she had carefully prepared for me, to unpack. We had supper quietly together, then I went out for a stroll round the village. It had rained a lot the previous day, and now the air smelled really fresh. I decided to visit the cemetery. It's a very special place for me, particularly when it is all dark and silent. I needed to think things over. As soon as I arrived, the smell of the earth started to tickle my nose, as though all the corpses had fled it with their flesh and bones and given it a unique character. I was immediately drawn to a huge, beautiful marble tombstone. I could not help going over to it and caressing the cold marble. It was a very strange feeling, but it brought me a sense of comfort and peace.

And I suddenly thought how perfect it would be to defy death by bringing this place to life – in other words, by making love here among the tombs.

The sound of twigs snapping or of someone treading on leaves brought me out of my reverie. It might have been just my imagination playing one of its tricks, so I decided to stay quite still, until all at once I saw a light in the distance. I was frightened, but also extremely curious, so I walked towards the glow, as it grew bigger and bigger like a moon fallen from the sky. It seemed to be torchlight. Realizing I was not alone made me start to tremble, and I could feel the palms of my hands becoming moist, either through fear or excitement. Then I heard voices. I could see the outline of two men, and soon saw they were digging in the middle of the cemetery. One of them spotted me.

'Is there someone there?'

I went closer and stood in the light from their torch.

'I'm sorry, I heard noises and came to find out what they were.'

'This is no time to be visiting a cemetery, miss,' one of them said, waving the torch at me. 'Aren't you superstitious?'

'Why should I be? I don't believe in the living dead, if that's what you mean.'

Both of them laughed.

'We're digging the hole this late because there's a burial early tomorrow,' the other man explained.

Even from where I was standing I could see the bulge in his trousers. He saw me staring at him and said, 'Human nature can never stay still, even in places like this.'

He was looking me up and down, and as my eyes got used to the darkness I could see his expression change, though I couldn't make out his face very clearly.

I was wearing a long black skirt with a tight-fitting short-sleeved top of the same colour, and a pair of sandals. All of this was quite thin material, and I could feel the cool night breeze on my body. My nipples began to harden, and I could sense my breathing accelerate more and more. It was so silent in the cemetery I was sure the two men could hear it too, and even see my taut breasts beneath my clothing.

Then one of the men came up to me and started stroking my hair. He ran his hand over my face, and pushed two fingers into my mouth.

'Suck them!' he whispered.

I did as I was told. The other man had moved behind me, and started fondling my backside, his hands muddy from the wet earth. He lifted up my skirt and pulled off my panties, raising them to his face to sniff them.

'You smell of life all right, sweetheart!' he said hoarsely.

He bent down to pick up a clod of earth they had been digging, and started rubbing it hard into my buttocks. I was still sucking his companion's fingers, licking between them. His workman's hands had a strange tang to them: rough and salty.

The other one took down his trousers, seized his prick in his right hand and started to masturbate, shining the light of the torch on my backside.

'You've got an arse to die for, sweetheart!'

Even though I could not see his face, I could sense how frantically he was pleasuring himself, and felt all the more aroused. Then the two of them tied my hands with a piece of rope and one of them pushed me roughly to the ground, right next to the hole they had been digging for the next day's burial. My head was hanging over the side and I was looking directly into the bottom of the grave. I knew one of them had finished when an enormous hot jet spread over my stomach. The other man shone the torch right in my face, as if they were interrogating me.

'I bet you like it!'

All at once he seized my head and stuck his prick in my mouth. My wet, warm saliva made him come almost at once, spraying my palate and gums. I passed out.

I don't know how many minutes or hours passed. When I got up, my whole body was aching. Was it all a dream? I was completely alone, covered in mud from head to toe. Apart from that, there were no traces of what had happened, and no sign of any rope. I decided to go home.

31st March 1997

I spent the whole day thinking about what happened yesterday, while Granny sat knitting and occasionally glancing over at me, intrigued by how serious I looked, sitting there writing this diary. I was in a small armchair which is protected by a blanket because Bigudi the cat loves to get up on it and clean herself. Bigudi was in front of me, looking at me suspiciously because I had taken her favourite place. I picked her up, kissed her on the head and stroked her fur so that she would start purring: my favourite tune, so full of pleasure and satisfaction. I closed my diary to offer her room on my lap, but she preferred just to sit there stubbornly, watching me.

'It's going to rain again today,' I said to Granny, watching the cat clean herself behind the ears.

'That's good for the garden,' she replied, with a slight smile that hung around her lips.

Granny is always smiling. She's a wonderful woman who's almost six feet tall. During the Second World War she joined the French Resistance, walking through woods carrying secret messages in her baby's pram. I admire her for that.

I watched her intently as she crossed the wool from side to side. I have never known Granny with any other expression on her face than the one she has now. It's as if she had suffered from amnesia all her life, or as if I had lost my memory.

'Granny, did you have any lovers before Granddad?'

My question did not seem to surprise her. She answered me calmly without raising her eyes from her knitting.

'Your grandfather was the only man in my life. I married him because that was the thing to do in those days. But I learnt to love him. You have to bear in mind what they said in a film once: a woman without qualifications has only two options, either marriage or prostitution, and they come down to the same thing, don't they? I've never made love with another man, if that's what you mean, not even before I met your grandfather.'

'And if you could start all over again, what would you do?'

'Why, make love to as many men as I could, child,' she replied with a laugh.

So now I know where my liberal-minded character comes from. I got up and kissed her on both cheeks to thank her for her sincerity and the trust she had shown me.

'Ah! And you have my permission to write and tell me all the details about your lovemaking, sweetheart,' she said.

'I promise I will.'

1st April 1997

Esperanza, Esperanza, sólo sabe bailar chachachá.
Esperanza, Esperanza, sólo sabe bailar chachachá.

The radio in the taxi I took at Barcelona airport was on at full blast. I even had to shout at the taxi-driver to get him to understand where I wanted to go. It never occurred to him to turn it down. The taxi was full of religious knick-knacks, and there was the photo of some saint or other on the rear-view mirror. Even the dog with the nodding head on the back shelf had a cross hanging round its neck.

'So you're from *la France*? I could tell at once, mademoiselle. So, are you on holiday here?'

Poor guy, it wasn't his fault, but I didn't have the slightest desire to talk to him, so all I did was nod in agreement. He didn't seem to get my point, and went on chatting.

'I speak *un petit peu* the French. And also *speakin inglis*.'

'Speaking English,' I corrected him.

'Yes, that's right, *speankin inglis*,' he replied, proud of himself. 'When I was young I went to England to work as a cook. That's where I learned to speank the language. But that was many years ago, and I can't remember much any more. I still do the cooking at home, though. My wife can't complain. Every Sunday I make her a *fideuá*. It's not easy to make a decent *fideuá*, let me tell you.'

After he had told me all about his wife's favourite foods, what his children do, and what good children they are, let me tell you . . . and how well his daughters-in-law have been accepted in his village, I finally managed to say goodbye to the taxi-driver. I gave him a good tip.

It was late, but I thought I might still be able to catch up with my bank manager from the other night. I wanted to see him and make a start with what we never got around to at that dinner. When I gave him a call, I got his voicemail, so I immediately left him a message:

'Call me at any time.'

At any time? He's going to think either that something has happened to me, or that I'm crazy. Too bad. At least this way I'll find out if he's really interested in me.

At one in the morning – nothing. At two, still nothing. By three I couldn't stay awake any longer, and went to bed. At half past four I was still tossing and turning, unable to sleep a wink. At a quarter to five I got up for a pee. Five o'clock, and still I couldn't get to sleep! At a quarter past, I got out of bed and ate some chocolate mousse. Guess what? I still couldn't sleep. I realized it was never going to happen, so I got up looking dreadful and wanting sex so badly nothing my hand could do would calm the urge.

2nd April 1997

Because of the lack of sleep, I had a terrible day. I was in a bad mood all morning, and on top of everything else, I had to start the preparations for my trip to Peru. My workmates did not dare ask me what was wrong, but I was so pale that Marta, the secretary, asked me if I didn't need a shot of glucose from her bottle of Coca-Cola to give me a lift.

'I hate the stuff!' I told her, not lifting my eyes from my computer.

I was trying to write a fax to set up a meeting with a Peruvian company. 'Anticipating your prompt Coca-Cola, I remain yours sincerely,' I wrote. When I reread it, I was even more annoyed because I had to correct it.

'Please Marta, don't bother me any more, I just make mistakes,' I snapped at the poor woman. She left my office with a sigh, shutting the door silently behind her.

I couldn't send the fax. I checked the number to make sure I had got it right, and tried again. Finally it went through. I hope they reply soon. I've already set up several meetings, but I don't want to leave Spain until I know exactly what I'll be doing in Peru.

In the afternoon my boss, Andres, called me in to discuss how my plans were going.

'Well then my girl, how do you feel about your trip?'

Why does he always call me 'my girl'? Andres must be around sixty, and I'm thirty years younger, but we only work together. His attitude often makes me feel like a little girl. He's still got a good head of hair, going white now, and I'd wager that a few years ago he was quite a woman-chaser. Now, though, I bet the snail is back in its shell. So all he can do is adopt this fatherly tone.

'What's wrong with you today?' he asked, taking off his glasses and narrowing his eyes.

'There's nothing wrong, Andres. I had a bad night, that's all. Why are you all going on at me so today?'

'OK, let's leave it there. But remember, my girl, that I need you to see everyone on the list in Peru.'

'Of course. Don't worry. I'll sell my soul to the devil if need be. You know me.' Even I didn't believe what I was saying to try to reassure him.

'If things get tough, I'll send someone to give you a helping hand.'

I shot out of his office because it was getting late and I still had a lot to get through. I almost fell over a heap of files Marta had spread out on the floor, and collided with her desk. Just at that moment, my mobile sounded.

I was out of breath and even more annoyed than before – Marta noticed and kept her head down among her files – when I reached my office. But it was too late. 'Call 123 . . . New voice message,' the mobile told me. I was so nervous I made a mistake dialling my voicemail. My nerves play those kinds of tricks on me sometimes. Calm down, I told myself. Calm down, this isn't going to help.

'This is Cristian. You left me a message yesterday evening. I'm returning the call.'

My bank manager! I slid the door to my office shut and dialled him back at once.

'Hi Cristian, it's me.'

'That was quick!' he answered, surprised.

If you only knew how much I feel like fucking you, I thought.

'Well, I got back from France yesterday and wanted to know what you were up to. How are things?'

'I've got a lot of work, but fortunately I'm in a privileged position. I finish by mid-afternoon.'

'Lucky you! So what do you do with yourself all afternoon? You must have a lot of free time.'

I wanted to know more about him, and especially if he could fit me in somewhere.

'I work out. Go shopping. Sometimes I go for a drink with a beautiful woman friend . . . what are you doing later?'

Aha, that's good, I thought. He wants to see me.

'If you like, we can meet up. I don't know what time I'll be finished, but I could phone you as soon as I leave the office. How about it?' I asked.

'Fine. Bye.'

Just as I was leaving the office, the heavens opened. I hadn't brought an umbrella because the weather had been fine all morning, but the moment I stepped out into the street I became a Noah without an ark. It's always the same. Everybody started to run like crazy, jumping over the puddles of mud and water that had already begun to form on the pavements. I decided to go at my own pace. There was no point running: I had no umbrella and it was raining so hard I was bound to get drenched anyway. Besides, I like the feeling of wet hair when it's hot, and the smell of damp asphalt. The rain takes me back to when I used to visit my grandparents in the country as a little girl. And the summer holidays I used to spend with my friend Emma.

By the time I put the key in my front-door lock, I was soaked through. What I needed was a hot bath with lots of salts.

I threw all my clothes off in the corridor – even my bra was dripping. Then I went into the living room naked and put on a Loreena McKennitt CD: *The Visit*. I poured myself a glass of red wine and lit some perfumed candles in the bathroom. With a Shakespeare poem to a harp accompaniment playing in the background, I took a leisurely bath for about an hour. By the time I emerged, all my fingers and toes were wrinkled. It feels great! This is how I would like to die. I confess I've often imagined how it would be. I think it must be like a lengthy dream as we travel in towards our soul. The pain of death is what most frightens people. But death cannot be pain, because pain is physical and death is the definitive state when we have 'shuffled off this mortal coil'.

I've got my own theory about what happens to us when we die. We are pure energy, and on our death our atoms mingle with the rest of the Universe. Our little bundle of energy becomes part of the energy of the Cosmos. There's no heaven and no hell. And that's how I feel when I'm making love. I can feel my energy flowing into that of the other person, and I'm taken on a journey until I fuse with the Cosmos. The energy of my orgasm is a tiny part of myself that mingles with the Universe. When I collapse exhausted after sex, I gradually return to my human state. My body cells go on a journey to the stars, where they are dispersed forever, caught up in a tumult of energy that I cannot control but which is constantly calling me.

I think that's why we want to repeat the experience time and again. To try to understand it better. Not that I ever really understand anything. It's a *petite mort* I am eternally trying to domesticate. That's what we French poetically call our orgasm. Every act of lovemaking is my way of getting closer to this sense of ecstasy. But I can never grasp it properly, which is why I'm condemned to repeat the experience endlessly, to try to comprehend it. In other words, it's a mountain with a huge abyss into which I never quite fall, with one foot on the ground and the other in mid-air. And my body swings like a pendulum between the human and the divine.

It was eleven at night. When I got out of my bath, I had a text message from Cristian.

'Rain, champagne, your skin ... why do I feel so aroused?'

Cristian sure knows how to arouse someone himself with a suggestive message like that.

'When we meet, I'm determined to find out what those three dots mean,' I texted him back.

'Good night ...' he wrote, to show he had got the message.

No doubt about it, he's a clever guy.

I went to bed, but had difficulty sleeping. His messages had set my hormones racing, and I didn't know whether I would have the patience to wait until the next day.

3rd April 1997

I arranged to meet Cristian in a bar after work. I knew nothing was going to happen because I have my period.

Shit. It came on this morning without warning. It was early, as though my body were telling me it was tired and needed to take things easy. I should have cancelled our date, but couldn't. I was too keen to see him again.

After an interesting conversation over a few glasses of French red wine and some tapas, he invited me to the most fashionable disco in the city. When I see someone dance, I can tell straight away whether they are sensual or not. In Cristian's case, there's no doubt: he dances really well. And ... rain, champagne, his skin ... I'm gone.

Gone into a parallel world, a dreamless *huis clos*, in which my body melts eternally into a velvet robe, where pleasure goes beyond all limits and becomes tiny diamond drops in the corners of my eyes, where his fingers brush against me like butterfly wings, and the hands of the clock whirl round twenty-four hours with me caught up in them.

It all began with some hectic dancing, while we chatted and flirted with friends Cristian met up with in the disco. Our drinks of rum with Coke or lime were stronger even than the music blaring out from the loudspeakers. I was dancing on an endless thread of silk like a tiny tightrope walker, caught between feeling his swollen penis rubbing against me inside his tight Italian trousers, and the burning glances a stranger was throwing at me as I whirled seductively round. I could feel myself falling, losing control. I wanted to feel I was alive.

'Tame me,' I whispered to him with my eyes.

I am looking for someone special, a man who can express his feelings through sex. Back at Cristian's place, after an exotic fruit punch, I lost all my senses and found myself spreadeagled beneath a penis that looked far too big for me, but which was impossible to resist. I took three hours to explore every part of this fleshy vibrator with my mouth. Underneath the sheets I looked like a comic-book ghost; I could hear him saying I was driving him crazy with pleasure, and sucked and chewed at him until I felt his prick had explored every single filling I had collected since I was a little girl.

I had two things blocking my suppressed sensuality. Embarrassed, I quickly removed one sitting on the bidet; he put the other one on me with an expert touch. I let myself go, like a puppet in the hands of a higher power, too aroused to do anything at all.

His unshaven cheeks did not bother me as in an act of generosity he ran his face down to the centre of gravity of female pleasure, forgetting that what is most intimate should be earned, not stolen by force. But he had extrasensory perception, and that made him dangerous: all I could do was approve with my eyes all that he did.

He wasn't bothered either by my unkempt bush, a sign that not everything can always be planned, that everything comes together because that is the way it's mean to be. The smell in the room was like no other.

'Attar of roses,' he said, reading my mind.

Everything faded into one. Rum from the night before at the disco, the fruit punch, now essence of roses at dawn, the black bottle of Armani each time I went to the bathroom, the *bagnoschiuma* from a Melia hotel in Italy on my skin when I took a quick shower, not wanting to miss a single moment of his presence. All these odours and tastes coursed through my veins, while at the same time my blood cells were reproducing at vertiginous speed.

He was crushing my mouth because that was the only way he knew how to kiss me, and I could feel I had a cut on the inside of my lip. He kissed me like a dog licking its returning master when it realizes it hasn't been abandoned. He bit my neck like a cat on heat, which prepares for the reproductive act with a ritual of this kind. All this gave me goose flesh. The hairs on the back of my neck stood on end for hour after hour.

In the morning I found myself, exhausted but satisfied, on a black rug that contrasted sharply with the pale white skin of my body.

He dropped me early outside my place. I walked up to my apartment like a zombie, suddenly finding I had been changed against my will into a kind of Marguerite Duras, obsessed forever with a lover who drove her mad at the age of fifteen, and condemned ever afterwards to write about a passion that imprisoned her in that moment of adolescence.

I Go On A Trip

Dear Granny,

I'm writing you this letter to tell you that last night I saw the stars. In close-up. Yes, so close I could almost reach out and touch one, but it was a shooting star and it vanished. What I mean Granny is that I had one of the best lays in my whole life. I thought you'd be pleased to hear it. I went to bed with a man I had only seen twice, and had met by chance in a bank. But it was magic. The first time, nothing happened between us. I think that was because neither of us wanted it. But last night I slept with him. We went out for a drink and then to dance. Afterwards, he took me back to his place. He's got a great apartment, a loft, with a huge balcony running all the way round it. All he needs is a big fat cat like Bigudi to prowl from one room to another. I'd warned him I wasn't prepared for sex that night because I had just got my period. So it was all a bit unhygienic … I felt so embarrassed. But he told me that sometimes

41

we cannot help ourselves, and we have to accept it. So I went with it. Were you as filthy when you were a young woman? I've lost my bearings. I can't stop thinking about him. Am I so frivolous that I'll fall in love with a man just because he is a great fuck? I don't like that idea, Granny. What am I to do? If he calls me, should I see him again? Give me some advice, please. I need it.

A big, big kiss. Take care of yourself.

YOUR LITTLE GIRL

PS: I'm going to Peru next week. I'll send you a fax with my address there if you want to write to me. And a postcard from Machu Picchu, I know you'll love that.

6th April 1997

Four o'clock in the afternoon, and Cristian hasn't called or sent a message. Shit! I couldn't stop thinking about him all day. Could I be falling in love? Why doesn't he get in touch? Didn't he enjoy spending the night with me? If he didn't, why did he say it had been sublime? Empty words . . . ?

My brain was racing, and I couldn't help thinking about what he might be doing on such a sunny day. Was he on the beach with those same friends we met up with in the disco, laughing at the way I spread my toes just after I've come? Just imagining that possibility crushed my self-esteem. He could at least have called to say he enjoyed the night with me. We women like to be told these things over and over. And I'm no different from anyone else. Cristian doesn't seem to be much of a psychologist, and that disappoints me. It's not as if I'm asking him to be the father of my children, but he could at least be polite enough to stay in touch. But who cares? If he can't be bothered to call, that means it wasn't worth it anyway.

Just in case, I looked for a book that's always useful in moments like this. It's called *How to Break Your Addiction with Someone*, by Howard M. Alpern. In it, the author says: 'Some people die due to abusive relationships. Do you want to be one of them?'

What am I doing? I've only ever met him twice. Perhaps all he wanted was to make love to someone without any complications, and there I was. Why am I getting into such a state over this guy?

It's hard for me to admit, but I really want to go to bed with him again. I'm going to read the book, and follow the advice in the final pages. I'm not falling in love, I'm not falling in love, that's what I've got to tell myself.

At one in the morning, I woke up sprawled on the sofa with the book over my face. I had fallen asleep in an awkward position, and my whole body hurt. I dragged on my slippers and went to the bathroom, still groggy, to clean my teeth. I've literally got the pages of the book printed on my right cheek. I was really annoyed with myself, and went to bed promising myself I would remove Cristian's phone number from my diary once and for all. A shooting star – that's all he was.

10th April 1997

'You need to leave. Right this minute!' Andres shouted at me, glasses in hand.

Every time he plays the role of heavy-handed boss, he

narrows his eyes as though he can't bear to face the person in front of him. He shouts, but he doesn't want to have to take responsibility for the astounded looks he generates.

Today he was sitting at his desk, drawing all kinds of shapes on the corners of the pieces of paper lying there: spirals, three-dimensional cubes, daisies. He goes over and over the lines so that in the end the whole sheet of paper turns into a black, meaningless mass. They'd make a good psychiatric test, I thought.

'But they haven't even replied about the most important interview,' I told him.

'I couldn't care less. I'm not bothered if you haven't packed your bags, or completed your planning, and even less by the fact that you've got your period. We've postponed this trip several times already. When you took on your job, you knew you'd have to be prepared to react immediately. Why on earth did I hire a woman? Why?' he asked Marta, who had appeared in the office doorway with some papers for him to sign.

Marta was trembling so hard she didn't even dare approach his desk. There's no doubt the boss was furious: there was a bright purple spot on either side of his nostrils, and he looked like a dragon about to spit fire and reduce us to ashes on the spot. I was as keen as Marta to get out of there, so I kept edging towards the door, but Andres was obviously determined to take it all out on me.

'I haven't finished with you yet,' he said. 'When you get to Peru, keep on at Prinsa. They're slowcoaches, and if you don't call them every day, they'll forget you exist. It doesn't matter how pushy you seem, get it, my girl?'

'Yes, Andres,' I muttered, watching him tracing yet more wavy lines on his sheet of paper.

He was pressing so hard that a few holes had started to appear.

'OK, now get a move on! Pack your bags, and get to the airport. Your flight's at five this afternoon. Marta has your tickets. Send me a fax as soon as you arrive. And good luck, my girl!'

I grabbed a taxi right outside the office, and it dropped me at home. There was a huge crowd in front of the door to the building, and I had to excuse myself several times as I pushed through the dozens of people waiting at the foot of the stairs.

'What's going on here?' I asked a dyed blonde who had a ring through her nose and was wearing bright fuchsia lipstick.

'We're waiting for Felipe from Office A, but he hasn't arrived yet, so we have to stand out here.'

Felipe is one of my neighbours. I don't know exactly what he does, but he has his business in the office downstairs. I've seen him several times, but only to say hello. I rushed up the stairs, quickly opened my front door, and started packing my suitcase. I hate doing that! Even though I had known about this trip for a month, I still didn't know what to take with me. I went through all my suits and in the chest of drawers counted how many bras and panties I would need. At the same time, I called Mercedes Taxi for them to send someone to pick me up. My apartment looked like a badly organized high-class boutique. I hate having to prepare a trip at the last minute. On top of everything else, I had to sit on my case several times to close it. What was the secret combination? What on earth was the number of the lock? I couldn't remember it! I was beside myself; the taxi was at the front door, and I had to take everything out of the first suitcase and put it all in another one. All because I couldn't remember the blasted combination. I hate myself for things like that. I'm completely hopeless, and they always seem to happen just when I'm most in a hurry.

My nerves were in such a state that I stood in front of the bathroom mirror and with a face like a Buddha on an off day I started to practise some abdominal breathing exercises designed to help me relax. They usually work. While I was looking for some condoms to put in my case, I came across a fax from my friend Sonia I hadn't yet had the time to look at. I told myself I'd read it on the plane. I took the lift down: walking upstairs is good for the gluteus muscles, but there's no point walking down. I ran into the same crowd of people waiting in front of the door to Office A.

While the taxi-driver was putting my things in his boot, I couldn't help asking the blonde I had seen earlier, 'Are you here for a job interview? Has he called you all at the same time?' I was hoping to find out more about Felipe.

'No, it's not that. We're here to rehearse. But he's the only one who has any keys,' she replied, as if it were obvious.

All at once I became very interested in what Felipe was up to. As I was getting into my taxi, I asked her again, 'What is it that you all do?'

The blonde girl beamed at me. A lanky young guy left the others to join in our conversation as I was getting in the taxi, shutting the door, and opening the window.

'We're all professional actors,' the blonde explained, lifting her chin proudly.

Then she added, as if to satisfy my obvious curiosity, or perhaps to whet my appetite for more, 'Felipe sells slices of life.'

The taxi-driver scowled at me in his rear-view mirror, giving me to understand he was parked in an awkward spot, and accelerated away.

Just before I got on the plane, and was about to switch off my mobile for good, I got a message. It was Cristian. 'Would you like to have dinner with me tonight?' My God, here I was leaving Spain with two huge un-answered questions: what sort of slices of life did Felipe sell? And what was I to do about Cristian? I'm so curious and impatient, I'm not sure I am going to be able to wait for an answer to them until I get back.

Several hours into the flight, as I was sifting through all my duty-free purchases in a plastic bag, I found I had to put up with the snores from a half-bald pachyderm sitting next to me. Disgusted, I turned to look at him, and saw with horror that his head was drooping ever closer to my shoulder. He'd better not lean on me! I thought.

I tried to keep my mind busy, because each time I fly I feel more afraid. I remembered Sonia's fax, and started to read it.

Dear Val,
I know it's ghastly and vulgar, but at least it will cheer you up today . . . Sonia

She'll never change. I've been friends with Sonia for three years now, and she has always given me the right message at the right moment. She works as product manager in a pharmaceutical laboratory, and is obsessed with getting promotion. When I first met her, she reminded me of Candy, the heroine in a Japanese animation film they used to show on French TV when I was small. Candy always wore miniskirts and knee-length boots. Sonia is just like her. Her skin is like bone china, she has enormous eyes set off by infinitely long eyelashes and a tiny snub nose covered in freckles. Her face is completely smooth, without a single wrinkle. She always wears sensible skirts and flat-heeled shoes, which make her shapeless body look like a stick. But inside, Sonia has always been pure fire. She has spent forever in a desperate search for the love of her life. And because she can never find him, she suffers from lengthy periods of depression. When she gets tired of seeing herself in such a state, she dedicates herself to making people laugh. Until she feels depressed again.

I began by counting the pages she had sent me. There were almost five of them: I don't know how she found the time to send such a long message from her office. The whole fax was a list of jokes about men, a kind of catalogue of their main mistakes in bed. A lot of it was nonsense, so I used the rapid-reading technique I had learnt at university to pick out the best bits.

After a while, I had read enough. Sonia was trying too hard to be funny. But at least her fax helped me forget the presence of the fat man next to me, who had woken up all of a sudden and was trying to read the pages over my shoulder. Our eyes met and a slight conspiratorial smile formed on his purple lips. I did not feel like responding.

Instead, I stared closely at the screen in front of me, which showed a map of the world and the position of our plane on it. We had already reached the American continent, and somehow that image helped me forget how anxious I had been in the days before I left Spain, struggling with Andres' bad temper and my obsession with Cristian. There is another adventure awaiting me.

Lima airport looked like a fruit and vegetable market. It was complete chaos, and as soon as I set foot on Peruvian soil I felt completely disorientated. It wasn't until I had been through passport control, changed some money to Peruvian soles and dragged my suitcase to the exit that I felt any better. As the doors opened onto the world outside, I was hit by an unpleasant wave of damp heat, which foretold sleepless nights drenched in sweat, and the inevitable gastric problems. I could hardly breathe, and there was a dreadful smell of rotten fruit. I looked around desperately for a taxi with air-conditioning, and finally saw one driven by a tiny little man wearing a natural linen shirt and a pair of combat trousers. He was constantly wiping off the sweat from his forehead with a handkerchief, then examining it as though he were panning gold. He waved his hand in my direction to show he was free. I didn't think twice, but went straight up to him.

'I'm going to the Pardo Hotel in Miraflores. Have you got air-conditioning in the car?'

'Of course I have. Get in, we'll be there in no time,' he told me, literally snatching the bag from my hands.

His air-conditioning consisted of several tiny fans placed above the driver's seat and pointed at the passenger. They revolved slowly and painfully with the sound of an enraged hornet. I made no comment. It was better than nothing.

The city of Lima is a giant slum where a lot of the houses seem on the point of collapse. Many of them have plastic sheets for roofs. It was nothing like I had imagined. I started searching desperately for any nice houses, an elegant villa, children in navy blue uniforms and long stockings coming out of a school somewhere, but I could not see any. Instead all I saw were tiny filthy faces, smeared with dried snot. The taxi-driver pointed out the sea and the city beaches. When we stopped at a light, he turned and warned me, 'But you're never to swim there, miss. All Lima's beaches are polluted. You have to get out of the city if you want to swim safely.'

I saw some huge rubbish dumps lining the beach, and was horrified to see people with their trousers rolled up to the knee searching for scraps others had thrown away. I felt so sick I had to turn my head away quickly so as not to throw up inside the taxi. I searched instinctively in my bag for my international vaccination card, and read all the dates on it. My taxi ride started to seem endless, especially as I didn't dare look out of the window again for fear of seeing more terrible sights right in front of my nose. At last we pulled up outside a hotel advertising luxury rooms, and as I was paying the driver, a hotel bellboy dressed in a red and black uniform and shiny shoes appeared.

'Welcome to the Pardo Hotel, miss,' he said in a very friendly way.

The hotel reception was expecting me, and they gave me the key to my suite, which looked onto the courtyard of the hotel as I had asked. At last I could get some peace and quiet. The room was beige, with a brown leather sofa in one corner. There was a huge, freshly made bed, and I collapsed onto it to try to regain some of the energy drained from me by the hours on the plane and the interminable taxi ride. Then I suddenly remembered the first urgent mission I had to accomplish: to get in touch with Prinsa.

I wasn't able to speak to the person I needed, so I left a message. Then I went down again to reception and talked to the girl who had greeted me when I arrived at the hotel. Her name was Eva, and she never seemed to stop smiling. She told me about the possibility of hiring a guide to visit the city.

'We have lots on our books, and they're all reasonably priced.'

Before I could say no, she pulled out a list and showed it me. I didn't have the slightest intention of hiring anyone, but my eye was drawn to one with the same surname as the Spanish novelist:

Rafael Mendoza
Tourist Guide
Press and Film Photographer

'Do you know Rafael Mendoza?' I asked Eva.

'Yes, Rafael is a good professional and an excellent photographer. Perhaps you'd like him to take some photos of Peru for you?'

As she said his name, she smiled broadly once more, and again before I could reply she was dialling his number.

I heard her leaving a message on his answerphone.

'Rafa, it's Eva from the Pardo Hotel. It's urgent, we've got some work for you.'

Promising Eva I would meet Rafa the next day, I took the lift back upstairs, feeling a need for sex I couldn't explain. Perhaps it was because of all the tension I felt during the long hours of the flight. When I reached my floor, I was just fumbling for the key in my bag when I heard a voice behind me.

'Good evening. What a coincidence we're in the same hotel!'

As I turned, I could see no higher than his lips, but I recognized him immediately just from them. It was the small, cynical mouth I'd seen dribbling in the seat next to me on the plane. The half-bald pachyderm had already pushed the key into the lock to his room. As I straightened up to get a proper look at him, he went on, 'Would you like to come in and have a drink?'

I surprised myself by saying yes, that was very kind of him, and yes how odd we were both in the same hotel, and by then the door was shut behind me. He asked me to take a seat on the sofa, which was exactly the same as the one in my room. The only difference was the colour of the walls, which were a garish yellow, matched by the curtains.

'What would you like? Champagne, red wine . . . ?'

'A whisky,' I replied automatically.

'On its own or on the rocks?'

'On the rocks, please.'

The pachyderm rang room service for the ice. He poured himself a glass of champagne, and started to question me on why I was visiting Peru.

'I work for an advertising agency,' I explained, trying to be friendly.

In fact, he seemed a decent enough person; it was just because he was so fat that I had taken against him. For a few seconds, I felt guilty.

'What about you?' I asked.

'I work for a phone company.' He told me its name. 'I'm a computer specialist, and I'm here to sort out some programs for our Peruvian office. Did you know our company has invested two billion pesetas in Peru?' he asked me, like a teacher trying to find out whether his pupil has studied properly for an exam.

'Yes, I had heard that. I know that since the end of the Shining Path guerrillas more and more foreign firms are investing in Peru. That's bound to be good for the country. I've read that your company's investment itself represents almost half of the total money invested here, doesn't it?'

I could tell by his look I had scored top marks. There was a knock at the door. The pachyderm took the ice bucket from the waiter, and shut the door with his left leg. Quite agile for someone his size, I thought.

He handed me my glass of whisky, still staring me in the eye.

'How long are you going to be here?' He wanted to know everything.

'About a fortnight. It'll depend on how long it takes me to see all our clients. Sometimes they cancel a meeting or postpone it, so all my planning gets in a mess.'

I asked him for another glass of whisky. The pachyderm, whose name was Roberto (that's what it said on his business card, which he gave me as if it was his most precious treasure) served me another large one. I began to drink it in rapid sips.

The drink started to have an effect, and I could feel a warm glow spreading up my legs until it reached my groin. A hot sensation spread up my spine and back. As Roberto went on talking, I slipped off my top and bra. Astounded, the pachyderm suddenly halted his monologue. Then he flung himself at my nipples, and chewed at them as if he was trying to let the air out of a balloon. I felt like a rubber bone being played with by a puppy. He lifted his head – the dribbling had started again – and began to twiddle my left nipple as though he was trying to find the Top Twenty radio station. I hate that kind of thing, but I let him get on with it. I knew what I was letting myself in for when I agreed to go into his room.

Then he started fumbling at the lower part of my body, getting his podgy fingers stuck in the elastic of my panties. In the end I had to take them off myself, but the pachyderm saw this as an invitation to penetrate me immediately, and slid his hand between my legs and shoved all five fingers up me, like a bank robber hiding his loot in a chimney. He really was clumsy, and his face was bathed in a clammy sweat. I was thinking this was not going to be a great deal of fun. He finally started taking his own clothes off, but just to show what a beginner he was in this kind of thing, he left his socks on.

Seeing him standing there like that I could hardly stop myself laughing. I searched unenthusiastically for his prick, but the rolls of fat seemed to be covering it entirely. He would have to find some way of lifting all those tons of flesh, or fucking was going to be impossible. Without more ado he roughly released his tiny thing from a grubby pair of briefs, thrust it in me roughly, pushed me down onto the bed, and started humping away. I felt I had to let him have a go. His face was smothered in the pillow, and his hands were clutching my buttocks. He was pulling me so tightly to him I was frightened I might suffocate under all that weight.

I decided to take the initiative. I shrugged my way out from under him. He looked at me in an extraordinary way, like a paid assassin. He did not even ask if anything was wrong.

'What are you doing? I was just about to come,' he growled.

'Lie on your back,' I told him.

Although he didn't appear to like my tone of voice, he obeyed. He turned onto his back and lay there, with his feet slightly raised, like a dog wagging its tail in the hope of being stroked.

'I can see you like to be told what to do, my little fatso,' I thought, smiling down at him. 'You were pretending to be so macho, but what you really like are dominatrixes. You only had to ask.'

I stood up on the bed, turned round so my backside was in his face, then sat on his tiny exclamation mark. He began to shout encouragement, like a football trainer on the touchline.

'Yes, yes! Go on! Oh, that's good!' he barked.

'You're going to see what a real Frenchwoman is worth,' I told him, turning my face to his.

'Yes! Oh, yes!' I could tell by the contortions on his face he had come.

A few moments later, I did too.

I jumped off the bed at once, and went to the bathroom to see what a mess he had made of my hair and make-up. Then I went back into the room to get dressed. My little pachyderm was lying in a lifeless heap. It wasn't that amazing, I thought to myself. As soon as I was dressed, I searched for the cigarettes in my bag, and lit one. I stared down at him, wondering how on earth someone like that could have given me pleasure.

'That was fantastic!' Roberto eventually managed to dribble.

The few strands of hair on the sides of his head were completely soaked with sweat.

'I hope we can do it again sometime.'

In reply, I smiled and left the room. No two ways about it, our bodies speak for themselves. And I use mine to communicate with people. Besides, today I did a good deed. My little pachyderm must have lost at least a couple of pounds, and I myself am that much closer to the finishing line of my personal marathon.

I Go Native

12th April 1997

When I opened the door and saw him standing there in his black-and-white-check imitation Faconnable shirt, I wished I were a draughts piece so I could run up and down his body. He immediately made me think of a game with some rules that could be more easily broken than others.

Rafael was as beautiful as a god. He had long, thick black hair which he gathered in a ponytail, and while he spoke he was constantly pushing rebellious strands behind his ears. His skin was dark olive, with a sheen that half the forty-year-old women who spend their lives sunning themselves on beaches around the world would die for.

Rafa was not bothered about the colour of his skin. Nor was I. But I have to admit that his origins did fascinate me from the start. His teeth gleamed like ivory, and for a second I felt as if I was on safari and had met an African elephant.

After he had told me his charges for acting as my tour guide for a few hours a day, and for taking some photos of the most interesting sights in Peru, I invited him for a wild weekend where his physical safety would be in great danger. He knew that, but I think he was willing to take the risk. I did not really need a guide, but hired him anyway.

14th April 1997

I love the intensity of our encounters. Rafa makes me feel happy in a way he probably does not even suspect. He motivates and inspires me.

The first time we met, I wondered if his skin was salty or not. Later, I discovered it smelt of vanilla, like the pods used to add flavour in cooking.

When we made love this morning, he spoke to me in Spanish, not in Quechua. I think this shows a timidity he is careful to hide: by speaking in what is not his native tongue, he distances himself from the enormous urge he feels to have me; the sound of his words bounces off the walls of the room and attacks my body, which shrinks each time one of them enters my ears and tickles my Eustachian tubes, weakening my resolve. I can never say no to him. After we have made love, I am always stained in words, my mouth is filled with imaginary shreds of coca leaves the two of us have chewed together, and my hair shines like never before. So does his. During our love-making sessions, he always wears it loose, and as it touches my body it's like a soft chamois leather.

I love how sensual his lips are, and while I am licking his big toe it excites me to watch how he reacts with pleasure, trying not to laugh, as his body wriggles on the spotless white bedsheets. I nibble at his heels, like a puppy playing with a slipper. The sound of the head-board against the wall must tell our next-door neighbour that we are indulging in reproductive activity most couples would be jealous of, but it's not the wild noises of some animal possession like a Cro-Magnon man and his mate, but something much more subtle, which gives me goose bumps. I often find myself thinking of Roberto, my little fat friend.

Rafa often plays at covering my body in marmalade, because I have never liked it and we store the extra pots from breakfast in our minibar. First of all he licks me with his small, pointed tongue, then he puts it in my mouth. The warmth from his mouth contrasts with the cool marmalade. His skin is smoother than Italian marble, and this has been the first time I've had a com-pletely hairless body at my mercy. I feel proud to have such a wonderful specimen in my bed.

Today, after all our foreplay and moments of delight, he took off his condom, which by now was full to burst-ing, and left it by the bedside. I suddenly remembered the mistake many men make when they leave their condoms in full view of anyone, but I forgave him this once. On the contrary, I smiled over at him for the gift of crystal-clear semen he was making me. I picked it up between two fingers and sniffed at the tiny bundle, hoping to find the typical smell of sea water and egg white, but the only odour I could detect was that of latex dusted with a substance called SK70, which, according to the publicity on the box, does wonders for sensitivity.

When I came out of the shower, I wrapped myself in a

brand new electric blue towel, which unfortunately left little balls of material all over my body. As I stood to look at myself in the mirror, I observed with horror that several of them had even got into my most private parts. When he saw what had happened Rafa laughingly introduced his fingers into all my hidden corners, with all the assurance of a plastic surgeon changing my features completely. He picked off the bits of fluff as if he were taking out splinters. Today I felt like Fort Apache besieged by the Indians, whose chief was Sitting Bull.

'You're very beautiful, boss,' he told me softly.

And you're my very own totem pole, I thought.

18th April 1997

It was night-time, and Rafa was driving me to the most dangerous hills surrounding Lima. When I asked him to take me there, he stared at me and said, 'OK, boss, but on condition you put up your hair and hide it, so they won't see you are a foreigner. And I'll take a gun just in case, and we'll keep the doors locked. Don't even think of getting out of the car. Got it?'

'Got it,' I replied, looking serious.

I don't like wearing my hair up. I never liked having ponytails, plaits, or anything like that. I have a complex about my ears. At primary school they used to call me Jumbo, because they stuck out even from my beautiful long hair. God knows, children can be cruel. Fortunately, when I was ten my mother noticed and had my ears pinned back. I spent a whole summer on the Côte d'Azur wearing a scarf that covered my head completely. Everybody would ask my mother if I had a fractured skull or was suffering from cancer. In reply, she would cross her fingers to ward off the possibility I might have to endure one or other of those dreadful traumas. Anyway, I don't think the surgeon was particularly good, because my ears still look like cauliflowers, and I'm still embarrassed by them.

The road to the hills – if it could be called that – was covered in earth and showed there was heavy traffic along it. Our car was being thrown around like a ship in a storm, but I did not feel in the least bit frightened. On the contrary, I love it when the adrenalin kicks in. Besides, it excites me to know I have an armed man sitting next to me.

In the distance we saw the feeble lights of some shacks that seemed to be clinging to the top of the hill.

'Stop the car!' I ordered Rafa.

'What?' he said, slowing down and turning his head in my direction.

'Stop the car here!' I almost shouted at him. In the darkness I could not see how astonished he must look, but I could imagine it.

'If I stop now, I'll never get the car moving again, boss.' Rafa tried to be as firm as possible.

'We'll push it.'

My solution did not seem to convince him, and he paid me no attention. So I grabbed the handbrake and pulled it up sharply, without worrying about the consequences of what I was doing.

'You're crazy, boss, we could have an accident!' Rafa shouted at me. He pushed at my arm, preventing me from getting the brake fully on. The car came to a shuddering halt.

'What's wrong?' he asked me, almost angry at what I had dared to do.

'I want you to make love to me right here.'

'What?' he said, his anger changing to laughter.

I could see he understood what I meant, but could not bring himself to believe I could be so crazy.

'Make love to me here, in the middle of the road,' I said, struggling to open the car door.

This was difficult because the car was on a slope, and it took me several attempts to actually get out. I leapt out as if I were somehow gravity-free, and stood in front of the headlights so that Rafa could see me all the better. Perhaps that would arouse his desire. The countryside had a rather hostile look, and to make things worse, there was complete silence. Not a sound. Not a bird singing anywhere. A few moments later, Rafa got out of the car as well, and came and stood behind me. He pushed me down against the car bonnet with one hand, and lifted my blouse. I could feel the tips of his fingers running up and down my back, drawing little figure-of-eight patterns. The sign of infinity. The language of bees. From time to time he moistened a finger with his tongue, and started to move further down my back. Impatient, he undid my jeans button, and they fell around my ankles. Then he used two hands to lift my buttocks to the height of his prick, which was erect in the darkness as if invoking the Almighty. At that very moment, images from a horror film I had seen at university flashed through my mind. It was called *The Myth of Kzulu*. It was the story of a monster with a huge member which raped all the virgins it came across. They all died impaled on this gigantic prick. We used to go and watch this kind of horror film before our exams, to relieve the pressure. Perhaps now deep down I was anxious, and that was why I wanted to provoke Rafa.

Rafa began thrusting away, and as I too began to groan, I could sense he was about to climax. I did not stop him. I liked the idea he couldn't help himself. And he came. A few seconds later, I could feel myself coming too. I remembered how Cristian had become a shooting star, and thought of all the other men in my life, even those I had not met yet. I had never seen things so clearly. I let out a cry that they must have heard in all the silent shacks perched up on the top of the hill.

'Take photos of me like this, with my jeans down.'

Rafa did not need asking twice. He used his powerful flash, and turned his third eye on me.

'Smile,' he said, coming up close.

I adopted different poses, happy to be a model for a night.

'Let's go!' I told him when I had had enough.

We both got back into the car and, after revving the engine a few times, we managed to set off again. When we reached the tiny village on the top of the hill, we had a spectacular view of Lima. A swarm of kids surrounded the vehicle and ran after us. We came to a stop for a minute.

'Take some photos of the city,' I asked Rafa. 'And of the kids, could you?'

'Yes, boss. But you stay still, please! I don't want any

problems with these people. Can you see how they're staring at us?'

More and more people were coming out of ramshackle wooden and cardboard bars, curious to discover who had strayed into this territory reserved especially for the poor, the have-nots.

I could see satellite dishes on some of the shacks.

'How can they have TV dishes? I haven't even got one at home in Spain!' I felt completely bewildered.

'The Government has supplied them with electricity and water. It may seen unbelievable, but it's true. There are even buses that come up here. Private ones. So people can get up and down to the city for half a sol. A lot of the women sell fruit down in the city centre during the day, then come back up here at night.' While he was explaining this, Rafa was taking pictures of the children all round us.

They were having a great time, grimacing and sticking out their tongues.

'Take a photo, Rafa.'

'That's what I'm trying to do.'

At that very moment, I realized the flies on my jeans were still undone. I was struggling to do them up when I felt several tremendous blows on the sides of the car. Looking up, I realized that the hostile-looking crowd were trying to tip the vehicle over.

'Hold on tight, boss, we're getting out of here,' shouted Rafa.

He threw the camera onto my lap and slammed the car into first gear.

The crowd pulled back, and soon all we could see in our rear-view mirror was the dust of the road.

'Did you manage to get some photos?' I finally asked, as we were drawing near the hotel.

'Yes, boss. But just so you know it, it was complete madness to go up there. It could have ended very badly.'

'Yes, Rafa, you're right.'

Not Nice

19th April 1997

In spite of the tremendous shock we got last night, today I was full of life and felt great . . . apart from stomach cramps. A call from the company I had to visit changed my schedule completely. The marketing manager was expecting me in Trujillo, a city some five hundred kilometres north of Lima. I had to take a plane to get there.

'The manager will see you at two o'clock,' his secretary told me.

I barely had time to get to the airport, catch the plane, and arrive in time for my appointment.

I wanted to take Rafa with me, but he was finding it hard to get up. I dug him in the ribs several times, and after a lengthy shower, we sped to the airport in a taxi. The taxi-driver looked scared, and must have thought I was mad when I told him I was in a real hurry. Time for him obviously meant something different.

'I don't care if there are other cars in front of us. Drive

on the pavement if you have to. Don't worry about the police. Everything is covered . . . so just get on with it!'

At the airport we had to join a long queue. I thought we'd never get there in time, but eventually we found a flight and I relaxed.

After we had taken off, a really pretty air stewardess came to offer us lunch, which neither Rafa nor I could stomach.

'Do you mind if we take some photos in the plane?' I asked Rafa.

'Are you a photographer then?' the stewardess wanted to know, as she passed by with her trolley to take away the food neither of us had touched.

'Yes.'

She smiled at him shyly.

'She fancies you,' I whispered in Rafa's ear.

'How do you know?'

He seemed upset. It's normal for Rafa to attract women. He is a very handsome guy, although he's on the timid side.

'Female intuition.'

'Does it bother you?'

Why on earth should it have bothered me? I'm not exactly a jealous woman. On the contrary, I see it as a compliment if a woman is attracted to a man who is with me. And besides, how can I ask a man to be faithful to me when I sleep with anyone I want? I felt like telling him what had happened with Roberto the afternoon I arrived in Lima. But I had too much respect for him. I did not know how he would take it – I was afraid what his reaction might be. I can understand that not everyone is prepared to accept my philosophy of life.

'Not at all! I'm not a jealous woman, you know that,' was all I said to him.

After almost an hour's flight, we arrived in Trujillo. Rafa and the stewardess exchanged phone numbers because, according to her, she was looking for a professional photographer for her nephew's first communion.

The first thing we saw at the airport were signs saying there was an outbreak of cholera in the city. Wherever I go it seems this plague follows me, but according to my tropical diseases expert, it does not affect Europeans because we are not malnourished and our gastric juices kill off the cholera bacteria. It is still better, though, not to drink tap water or put ice in drinks.

We went directly to my appointment, which didn't go as well as I had hoped. Afterwards, to try to calm my nerves, we visited the city. From the surrounding countryside, I discovered that Trujillo is situated in the middle of a desert covered in fields of asparagus. Most of the crop is exported to Spain. Faced with these fertile dunes I suddenly felt angry and sad. I knew that my meeting with the Prinsa marketing manager meant my visit to Peru was almost at an end. I had got the interview I wanted, and there was no point staying on much longer. Rafa did not know this yet. I was afraid to tell him. Always my same problem: putting off things I don't like doing. Obviously, I'm not in love with him, but I feel very tenderly towards him.

Night of 21st April 1997

'Is there anyone there? I'm here! Please, someone get me out of here! I'm choking to death.'

In the midst of the most complete darkness, I was searching for a light to guide me. My whole body was aching, especially my legs. I could not make any sound. My jaw was locked open.

'Somebody help me!'

I could not move. I had lost all sensation in my limbs. It felt as though I had been buried in a coffin. But I was not dead.

Perhaps this was a kidnapping, and they had put me in a hole like the ETA people do. Why? This could not be real. I have nothing to do with the Basque problem. Anyway, what the fuck was this? I was in Peru, not Spain. I had just met with the marketing director of Prinsa Ltd. So what was going on? Could it be Shining Path?

'I'm a French citizen, resident in Spain.'

I try to remember: Guzmán is in jail, all the other Shining Path leaders have been caught too, it's been some time since there have been any other attacks. So it couldn't be them. It did not make sense. Perhaps it was those kids from the hills who were keeping me hostage. But it couldn't be that, either. If my memory served me right, we had escaped from there unharmed. So this must be a punishment from God for all the many sins I have committed in my life. But I haven't ever hurt anyone. All I was after was a bit of pleasure.

'Get me out of here! If I calm down, will someone come? Somebody reply, I can't take any more!'

I felt as though I were running out of air. I began to feel claustrophobic and sick. I must have been drugged, because I felt very dizzy. I wanted to scratch my nose, but I couldn't even lift my little finger. I tried moving my eyes, but I was like a blind old horse.

I heard a noise. Footsteps, voices. I felt so bad I no longer knew whether it was my imagination or if somebody really was approaching me.

'I'm here!'

I listened intently. It seemed as though they had heard me. But what was happening? I heard a tremendous crash, and felt myself being buffeted on all sides. An earthquake? I decided I knew what it must be. I was buried under the ruins of a building that had collapsed in an earthquake.

'Help!'

They must know there were survivors. They must have a rescue team with dogs, because in Peru an earthquake is a normal occurrence.

I tried to calm my fears. But all at once I felt more terrified than ever: what if I have been left paralysed? I could scarcely feel my body. I started to pray:

'Our Father who art in Heaven, hallowed be thy name, thy Kingdom come, thy Will be done, on earth as it is in heaven, give us this day our daily bread, and forgive us our trespasses . . .'

Light! At last I could see it. My prayer has been answered. The light was hurting my eyes, but finally I could see someone. Someone?

It was Roberto, my fat little pachyderm.

'Roberto! I'm over here! Help me, please! I'm so happy to see you! What's the matter? Why are you looking at me like that?'

Roberto was coming towards me in a menacing way that I was trying to decipher. He seized my head and lowered it to his open trouser flies. I did not even have time to sigh.

'Take that, take that, you shitty inflatable doll!' he shouted, sticking his syphilitic penis into my rubber mouth.

22nd April 1997

I woke up with a temperature and still feeling terrified in my bed at the Pardo Hotel. I had one question: did I have the Stockholm Syndrome for my sex-shop kidnapper?

The nightmare stayed with me most of the morning, and the fever as well. I had to concentrate, because there were lots of things I had to deal with today. Amongst them were: to find a flight back to Spain and to buy a postcard of Machu Picchu for Granny, as I had promised.

At Iberia they did the impossible: they found me a seat for the evening flight the next day. So I had twenty-four hours left in Peru. In the city centre I found an old street vendor who was selling all kinds of books and post-cards. He was very friendly, and I really liked the way he left his maize-paper cigarette drooping from his lip without every taking a drag from it. It was about to burn his mouth, but he did not seem in the least bit concerned. When I asked him about Machu Picchu, he brought out tons of images of the famous mountain: in colour, black and white, with views from every angle and inscriptions in every language. I felt sure I would find exactly what I was looking for. It seemed as if he had been collecting them since the day he was born, because some of the postcards were yellowing and smelt like books that have spent years untouched in some imposing library. I chose a colour postcard, paid him double the asking price because I felt so sorry for the poor man, and besides, what he was charging in soles was next to nothing – and, pleased with what I had bought, I extracted myself from the man's thanks and deep bows (as complicated as a Japanese diplomat's), and returned to my hotel.

Dear Granny,
   I'm sending you the small postcard as promised, but I have to confess I didn't see Machu Picchu. I didn't have the time. I've had my most important meeting, so now I'm heading back to Spain tomorrow evening. I'll call you as soon as I get home. Huge kisses. Your little girl.

I left the postcard at reception, insisting they send it as soon as possible. Eva told me not to worry. She said it would arrive safely, but could not guarantee how long it would take.

After that I rang Rafa, who was doing the morning aerobics programme from the beach that he helps film for Peruvian TV. We agreed to meet at the Mojito bar at midday. He left really early this morning, with an innocent kiss on the lips and a question as to how I was feeling. I had a few hours to work out how I was going to tell him I was leaving the next day.

I took my temperature again: 37.7. It had gone down a little, but I still didn't feel well, so I lay down for a while.

What on earth was I going to say to Rafa? How was he going to take it? Would he reproach me for not telling him sooner, and finding he was left with a kiss on both cheeks and no possibility of seeing me again? I spent the whole morning thinking it over, then when it was almost lunchtime I got up and put on some more make-up, to hide the dark lines under my eyes. I looked terrible, of course. I chose a jacket and ran out of the hotel.

The Mojito was full of beautiful people and the Lima jet set. It's the in place to have lunch and a drink. The restaurant is on two floors. Down below there are apple green tables and chairs, then there's a wooden staircase, just like the ones you see in Westerns, from the top of which a lascivious dancer in a cancan skirt, wearing impossible plumes on her head, scowls at all the cowboys leaning on the bar. The second floor of the Mojito only opens in the evening for customers. I looked around for Rafa, and found him drinking a Corona beer, Mexican style. He was chewing at the slice of lemon, and absent-mindedly staring at the marks his teeth had left in the skin.

'You don't look too good, boss!' he said, standing up and bringing over a chair for me.

'I think the trip to Trujillo wasn't a good idea,' I said, avoiding his eyes.

I signalled to a waiter.

'Are you sure there's nothing else?'

I could tell he suspected something. He was very nervous, and kept picking at the label on the beer bottle, tearing at strips until it was all off.

'The menu and another Corona, please,' I asked the waiter.

I lit a cigarette, and found myself trembling. Rafa noticed, but didn't say anything.

We ordered some cheese enchiladas, burritos – no hot sauce for me – and a bottle of the house red wine. Not exactly a Peruvian meal!

'I don't know if you should drink a lot of alcohol.'

Rafa had turned serious.

'I'll only drink a little. I think I'm not feeling well because yesterday was so exhausting. I'm feeling upset and worried because of those posters we saw about cholera in Trujillo. I feel nauseous, but I'm still hungry: that's a good sign, isn't it?'

I could not convince him. We ate lunch in almost complete silence, with Rafa occasionally shooting me meaningful glances, and telling me in a desultory way about that morning's work, the photos he had taken of me, and cursing the waiter for bringing us the food so slowly.

After the meal, I told Rafa I wanted to go back to the hotel. I wanted to be alone, and if my temperature did not go down, I was determined to call a doctor. He nodded in agreement, and as I was about to climb into a taxi, dropped a small yellow packet into my bag.

'Promise me you'll follow the instructions written on it.'

This took me by surprise, but I didn't feel well enough to react and ask what he meant. I nodded in my turn, and shut the cab door. When we pulled up at a traffic light, I glanced back and saw Rafa standing there looking sad. He was waving goodbye. I did not know why, but I felt sure I would never see him again. He knew it as well.

23rd April 1997

The doctor came to see me yesterday and diagnosed gastroenteritis. He also advised that when I got back to Spain I should visit the hospital to check I didn't have salmonella. I slept all afternoon, then tried to phone Rafa on his mobile, but it was out of service the whole time. I got up several times during the night, either to go to the toilet or because I was sweating and delirious. I remembered my encounter with Roberto and the nightmare I had had the previous night. The atmosphere in my bedroom became very stifling again, and I felt I was being buried. The whole room had a smell of rotten eggs, which I eventually realized was the effect of all my belching and retching.

This morning, though, I felt a lot better. My fever had gone as quickly as it had arrived, and I was looking forward to having breakfast and packing. I tried Rafa's number once more, but without success. Either he was angry with me, or he knew I was leaving and wanted to spare himself any dramatic goodbye scenes. I don't hold it against him. I spent the whole day working on reports about the clients I had visited, so that I didn't have to think too much.

A taxi was waiting for me at the hotel door, and I said goodbye to Eva, whom I had got on with right from the start. I'll miss her. I could not hide my feelings, and felt like crying. In the taxi I let myself go, and as the taxi-driver peered at me anxiously in his rear-view mirror, I wept and tried to dry my nose on a bit of toilet paper I found in my bag. Whenever I run out of Kleenex, I always make sure I have some toilet paper with me so I can dry any unexpected tears, or wipe my forehead and nostrils if they are greasy.

As I was looking for my ticket and passport at the Iberia check-in desk, I came across the small rectangular package Rafa had given me. It was very strange – it had a red seal with the initials R.M. I recognized Rafa's handwriting. The instruction was: 'Only to be opened on the flight.' I felt the package to try to work out what was inside. It was very hard. I decided to open it on the plane as instructed, though I was dying to find out what it was. I had promised.

There was quite a lot of turbulence on the flight, much more than on the way to Peru. It always happens just when the stewardesses are serving the meal. It's as though it were on purpose. I clung onto my glass of juice, which was sliding from left to right and then back again, like in a spiritualist session.

All of a sudden the red seat-belt light went on, and my heart started beating furiously. I dislike travelling by plane more and more. I needed to calm down with a cigarette, but I knew this would only infuriate the stewardesses and the other passengers, and that I would only be able to manage a couple of puffs. What I wouldn't give for them anyway! It was at that moment that I remembered Rafa's little package, so I took it out of my bag as carefully as someone holding a diamond worth a million dollars.

When I opened it, I discovered a tiny, beautiful box with a piece of paper folded inside it. It had a very short but unforgettable message on it:

Dear boss,
The treasure of love comes in small packages.
RAFA

Rafa, why was that all you wrote? I can't get enough of your words; is that all you had to say to me? I read the lines over and over again, and realized what a profound message the little box contained. The tears I started to cry were completely different from the ones I had shed in the taxi on the way to the airport. This time I was sobbing and sighing in a warm rush that was like a raging torrent. I could not remember ever having cried over a man like that in my life before. But was I really crying for him, or for those moments of happiness that are always unique and can never be repeated?

My U-Turn

Nobody was waiting for me at the airport. It was very early in the morning. My nose was completely stuffed up after having cried for seven of the twelve hours of the flight, and my eyes were as puffy as if two bees had stung me on both eyelids. I tried to console myself by thinking that I had at least left Rafa in good hands: he was sure to get together with the stewardess we met on the flight to Trujillo. Just thinking that brought a smile to my face.

The very first thing I did was light a cigarette. While I was waiting for a taxi at the terminal exit, I put my SIM card back in my mobile. My voicemail was bound to be full of messages, but I could listen to them all once I got home.

I had agreed to see Andres that afternoon, to tell him all I had done in Peru. First I would go home, lie down for a while, and then in mid-afternoon head for the office.

On the way into Madrid from the airport, I

rediscovered the civilization I had left behind only a few days before. I was fascinated by all the activity in the city. At a traffic light, I watched a man standing in front of the Gucci window, staring at the price of a pair of really high-heeled shoes. He was talking to himself, and had a nervous tic which meant his bottom lip kept shooting up and covering the top one. In a tearoom I spotted an executive pointing insistently at the largest cake on display, which was filled with custard. He was licking the left side of his lips in anticipation. I felt good. Everything here was much faster, and I could feel myself falling into the rhythm.

I've never got from the airport to my apartment so quickly: the city was still half asleep. Already, though, even before the city became a hubbub of noise, there was a thick, grey-looking cloud of pollution hanging over it, and the humidity was set to reach the highest levels. The wail of an ambulance reminded me I was back in Spain, and that I had left all the rest behind me. Sirens are different in every country, and are one way of realizing how foreign you are. And today I felt fine, but still in a strange country.

My mailbox was full of letters. Two of them caught my attention: a handwritten one, and a card with a blue sticker informing me that as I had not been at home, the package had been left at Office A. I must go and get it some time.

I opened the other letter and instinctively looked down at the signature. It was from Cristian. What was he doing writing me letters? I didn't feel like reading it there and then. Besides, he had not been there when I needed him, so I was still rather annoyed with him.

But I was pleased to be home. I said hello to all my bits of furniture. To me, they have a life of their own. I don't have a lot, but they all have great sentimental value. Above all, one painting, which is a reproduction of a woman's face by Modigliani. Everyone who has been in my place has asked if it was me.

'Me?' I said once, reacting with distaste.

'Yes, you look just like that woman with her smooth auburn hair, thin pink lips which might or might not be smiling, the large, strong nose and those eyes of yours which follow you round every corner of the flat.'

The girl in the painting isn't beautiful, but she is mysterious.

'She's like the Gioconda!' Sonia said the first time she saw it.

I collapsed onto my sofa, leaving my suitcase next to it, and rifled through all the other stuff that had arrived: telephone and electricity bills, publicity from a new beauty centre that makes china fingernails . . . I picked up Cristian's letter again.

Hi there Val,

I called you several times on your mobile, but it's switched off. So I've no idea where to find you. That's why I decided to write you this letter. Please reply, even if it's only to send me packing. I'd really like to see you again.

CRISTIAN

Let him suffer a bit! I crumpled up the letter and decided to throw it straight into the waste-paper bin. I had no intention of returning to Spain and immediately giving myself headaches over him. Instinctively, and to get over the bitter taste Cristian's letter left in my mouth, I headed downstairs to Felipe's office and rang the doorbell. He opened at once.

'Hi! I'm your neighbour on the first floor. Do you remember me?' I asked, with a broad smile.

I still had no idea what a godsend this meeting with Felipe would turn out to be. We met just as my life was about to change dramatically – exactly as he does with his clients.

Felipe is a strange-looking guy. He's short, with small feet and bow legs that make an O when he walks. He has long fingernails like a classical guitarist, thick, curly hair, and a small goatee that he grew deliberately to make himself look interesting. He always wears black or white, and white flip-flops. The first impression is of a very unremarkable guy, with his pale face and timid expression. He's incapable of coming out with a sentence without saying, 'Of course, of course,' and constantly stumbles over his words. His eyes are small and very dark, making him look like a tiny fox. In short, he's incredibly ugly.

'Of course, of course! There was a parcel for you, and since you weren't around, I signed for it. Hang on, I'll go and get it. Come in, come in, don't just stand there in the entrance,' he said shyly.

He went over to a desk and took out the parcel.

'I don't know how to thank you. If you hadn't been here to collect it, they would have sent it back, and I'd have had to wait ages for it,' I said while I was reading what was written on it.

'We neighbours have to help each other. Besides, I

81

already knew who you were. We've passed each other on the stairs a few times. You're French, aren't you?'

I was surprised he hadn't yet said a single 'of course, of course'.

'Yes, I'm French. But I've lived in Spain for a few years,' I told him, pleased I had received the gym equipment I had ordered on the Internet one night when I couldn't sleep a wink. Then I asked him, 'What about you? Pure-blooded Catalan, I suppose.'

'Yes, of course, of course. You can tell by the accent, can't you?' he said, looking down.

Curious, I stared down at the same spot on the floor, but could see nothing.

'And what do you do here?' he asked, moving his foot as if he were stubbing out a cigarette.

'I work for an advertising agency,' I replied, looking him in the face and waiting for some reaction.

He did not react in the slightest.

'An advertising agency. Of course, of course. That must be fascinating, I should think?'

He had thrust both hands into his trouser pockets. He seemed rather awkward, and still kept staring at the floor.

'Yes, it is sometimes. But I think what you do is much more interesting.'

At this, Felipe looked up suddenly.

'Ten days ago, when I was about to leave on my trip, I met a whole group of people outside your office. One of the girls told me they were actors, and that you sold slices of life. Is that true?'

I was determined to find out exactly what that 'slices of life' meant.

Felipe replied in all seriousness, 'Of course, of course. It sounds a bit strange, doesn't it? But that's right, I do sell slices of life. It's something new. I create stories and sell a character for a specified length of time. It's like a role play. People have lots of dreams. They'd like to be spies, pop stars, models, or hostages . . .'

'Hostages?' I said, surprised.

'Yes. And I make those dreams a reality. I create a situation, characters. I have some very good actors on my books, a screenplay, and everything seems real. Just like life!'

'That's really interesting,' I cried. 'How does it work?'

'I could explain, but it would take time. Why don't you come round tomorrow evening and we can talk about it at our leisure?'

'OK, I'll come round about eight. I have to work until then. Is that all right for you?' I was keen for him to say yes.

'Of course, of course that's fine. We're rehearsing all tomorrow afternoon anyway. If we finish early, I'll wait for you.'

We smiled and said goodbye, and I went back upstairs. I felt tired but once again my adrenalin had kicked in. Felipe had aroused my curiosity, and I could feel my whole body tingling with anticipation.

I tried to have a bit of a rest, then in mid-afternoon went to the office, in a mood to take on anyone.

Andres was waiting for me sitting on his throne, anxious to hear all the details of my Peruvian trip. I spent a few minutes chatting to my workmates, then knocked on my boss's door. I was keen to see him, because in spite of everything I rather like him.

'Come in, my girl!'

Every time I come back from a business trip, Andres gets up and kisses me on both cheeks. It's a habit, and also the only time I get to glimpse a tenderness in him that he usually hides at all costs. All the rest of the time he is the coldest man I have ever met. This time, though, he didn't embrace me, so I stood there with my cheek proffered like an idiot. And even though Andres was obviously pleased to see me, the atmosphere was tense.

'Hello Andres,' I said, deciding to sit down. 'Here I am with some new contracts, but Prinsa say they are still thinking it over.'

'You look tired, my girl. Did you have a good journey?' Andres asked with genuine concern, leafing through the reports I had brought him.

'More or less. All those hours in a plane, plus jet lag, are more than enough for anyone. But don't worry, I'm fine. What do you make of my work?'

'It looks fine, my girl. We can pursue Prinsa from here.'

'So, when is my next trip?' Even as I asked the question, I realized I'd hit the nail on the head.

Andres put down my reports and picked up his notepad with all the doodles on it. He started furiously drawing three-dimensional cubes, and then shaded in their sides with a pencil. He took his glasses off, and for some reason this familiar gesture made me realize he was about to give me bad news. His eyes were tired, and had enormous bags under them.

Everybody in the office knew already, but no one had said a word to me. I suddenly felt like a woman whose husband is being unfaithful to her, but is always the last to find out. I automatically reached up to smooth down my hair, but in fact I was feeling to see if my cuckold's horns were showing. As if on cue, my head started to ache, and that morning's sense of euphoria disintegrated into a kind of nausea that crept up from my stomach to my throat. I stared impatiently at Andres' trembling lips, but nothing came out.

'Come on, spit it out!' I almost shouted at him.

Andres had to take a deep breath to tell me what I already suspected. We were sitting opposite each other. I was breathless and he was visibly embarrassed at what he had to tell me.

'I'm really sorry my girl, but you're fired.'

I already knew that the firm was in the throes of a restructuring process, but it had never occurred to me I could just simply be fired. I didn't ask Andres to go into detail, because I was far too exhausted to start an argument. We agreed I would come back another day to sign the settlement papers, he kissed me on both cheeks, and I left his office in a daze. I went straight away to clear my desk, with Marta's help. She went on and on in a whisper about how unfair the situation was, telling me I should sue the company for unfair dismissal. We all knew there were more heads on the block, but mine was the first, and that was what hurt most of all.

I walked home stumbling along like a drug addict, still unable to take in properly what had happened to me. I needed to write, because I felt I was still under the toxic influence of what Andres had said to me. I picked up my diary to try to write down what I felt and understand it, but it was impossible. What I needed above all was to be with Cristian, to rediscover the inspiration I was lacking.

I recalled that, the first time we made love, I felt the need to record in writing all the sounds our clothes had made as they fell to the floor, to describe the way his tongue moved over all my body, the way his hands caressed my breasts, how tenderly he stroked my stomach, the scent of his breath on my face, like a small, familiar breeze that blew in whenever our bodies were crazy for each other, the happiness we shared with our orgasms, then the peaceful moments afterwards as we lay there entwined, the toes of his feet banging into mine as we both tried to get some sleep, how he clung onto me so I could not wriggle away to the far side of the bed. I had tried to write all this down the first time he had come inside me. But the memory of it had faded. Confused images whirled round my mind. I was tired out, and my life was about to perform a U-turn.

Slices of Life

25th April 1997

I spent the morning chain-smoking – my whole flat reeked of nicotine, and so did my hair, but I did not feel like taking a shower. I was simply filling in time until I met Felipe. I could have brought our meeting forward, but I wasn't in the mood to give explanations. He was the one who had to talk. I wanted to know everything about his precious 'slices of life', but if I told him I had just lost my job, he might be tempted not to say a word.

An hour before I was due to meet him, I jumped into the shower. I let the water cascade all over my face, just like I do on rainy days as I jump over puddles. Now it was goodbye puddles on the way to work; goodbye Marta, goodbye Andres. I'll miss you all.

I had to snap out of it. The first thing was to go and see Felipe. After that, I decided I would call Sonia and organize a hen party this weekend. And last but not least, I would try to find Cristian and spend the night with him.

After taking all these decisions, I felt more like my old self. I went down to Office A, and Felipe was obviously pleased to see me. He showed me in, then left me standing in the middle of the room.

'I think the best thing to do would be to show you the place first, then explain. Come on, follow me.'

His office was on three floors, linked by a spiral staircase. On the ground floor where we were, there was a computer, a fax, and loads of shelves filled with box files. Felipe took me up to the first floor, which was where he received his clients. It was very tasteful: all the furniture was wickerwork, and on the walls were hung several exotic paintings and photographs of people tied up on chairs, and of cemeteries and zombies . . . I could see a poster advertising a film starring Michael Douglas: *The Game*.

'I really like Michael Douglas,' I exclaimed.

'Did you like the film?' Felipe asked, with a smile.

'I didn't get to see it,' I had to confess.

'You should. Eight years before it came out, I was already designing "slices of life". But now, people think I must have copied the film to start my business, but in fact it's the opposite,' Felipe said, obviously put out. 'The film shows exactly what I do. *The Game* is the story of a multi-millionaire who is bored because he has everything. For his birthday, his brother has no idea what to offer him. So he decides to hire a company for a role play, in which Michael Douglas will play the central character. He has no idea of this. But then the game becomes dangerous . . . I do exactly the same for my clients, though I never let it become dangerous, get it?'

I nodded. His story fascinated me. We went down to

the basement, which was a huge, gloomy place with no windows, like a sort of bunker where unspeakable things might happen. The only furniture in the room was an enormous table with twenty chairs round it, and a plastic dummy dressed in a military uniform and wearing a gas mask. It was a truly scary place, with bare brick and cement walls. It looked like a hole in the floor that could collapse on top of us at any moment.

'This is where I bring my actors to rehearse all the scenes. That's why it's so big. We need space . . . space,' the echo of his voice repeated.

'Of course, of course,' I replied, realizing as I said it that I had adopted his own stock phrase.

Felipe did not notice, but went on with his explanations.

'I invent all kinds of stories: spy thrillers, horror, love stories . . . with varying degrees of danger, suspense and fear. My clients choose what kind of story they want, then they become the main character in it for a certain length of time: twenty-four hours, forty-eight, or whatever. All my actors wear a label with the name of the company on it, so that if the situation becomes intolerable the client can somehow get back to reality. They can see the label and realize that it is only a game. If they want to call a halt, they have a password they can use whenever they like. And before they start, they have to visit our psychologist to determine their state of mind. I also recommend they see a doctor for a health check. Anyone with heart problems is barred. I don't want to run any risks. We're a serious leisure company. As you see, I've thought of everything.'

'I understand,' I replied, intrigued. 'Tell me a bit more

about the people who want this kind of service, the prices, the stories themselves . . .'

'Of course, of course! My clients are all well off. The prices depend on how complicated the story is and how long it lasts, but in any case, it doesn't come cheap. This is a cutting-edge leisure pursuit. And as for the stories, they're of all kinds. I even have clients who ask me to make one up just for them.'

'Aha?'

'Of course, of course. My last client for example was a lawyer who wanted to be kidnapped for forty-eight hours by two women, and to be put into a hole in the ground. I invented the story especially for him. He loved it.'

'In a hole? People really are off their heads. As if there weren't enough kidnappings these days, you get a guy asking for it. I can't believe it!' I said, indignantly.

'What I didn't tell you was that the guy wanted two lesbians to make love in front of him down the hole he was being kidnapped in. I had to hire two prostitutes, because none of my actresses would do it.'

All of a sudden there was a strangely perverse, diabolic glint in his eye, which I found tremendously attractive. Felipe no longer looked like the fragile, shy fellow I had met the previous evening.

'Oh, he wanted two lesbians did he?' was all I could think of saying.

He stared at me for a few moments, then went on with his explanations as though nothing had happened.

'We once organized a medieval weekend for four people in a castle where Count Dracula appeared each night. They nearly died of fright,' Felipe said, bursting out laughing.

'I must say, I'd really love to be involved in a story like that. It must be great. But it would be far too expensive for me,' I said reluctantly.

'Would you really like to?'

He was staring at me again, with that perverse smile on his lips. He looked as attractive as before.

'Yes of course, of course. It must be really exciting!'

'Don't worry. You shall have your slice of life, and for you I'll put it on for free. But just remember this: once the client has agreed, he or she never knows at what moment the story is going to start. Are you up for it?'

'Yes,' I said, not taking him particularly seriously.

What on earth was I doing? I didn't know him at all, and here I was saying yes without the slightest idea of what I was getting myself into. Although I suspected it would be the typical kind of soap opera that has such an impact on people.

'Fine, but remember: when you least expect it . . .' Felipe said again, accompanying me to the door.

'OK! Good night, Felipe,' I said quickly, running back upstairs to my flat. Our conversation had really excited me, and I was amazed how a guy as apparently dull as him could suddenly become so attractive to me.

My body was on fire, and I needed the fire brigade. I called Cristian's number, but there was no reply so I left a message explaining why I hadn't been in touch for ten days. Twenty minutes later he called back, and we agreed to meet at his place.

As soon as I got there, we went straight to bed, without exchanging a word. Cristian took my head in his hands and started to lick my mouth, nose, eyes and neck. The sense of pleasure it gave me was like heartbeats pounding gently all over my face. Every so often he disappeared lower down my body, then brought back my own nectar for me to taste on my lips.

'Do you like it?' he asked, aroused to the limit.

'I love it. What about you?'

'Me too. It has a slightly sweet taste. It's like summer rain.'

I fell back, sated with pleasure, and took his moist penis in my hand. I started moving up and down, while he began exploring my secret cavern with his finger. I was enjoying myself, and so was he: we both came at the same moment, exhausted from the exotic positions we had got into, as if the intensity of our lovemaking depended on them.

A few hours later – I still don't know whether it was real or a dream – I suddenly found Cristian's buttocks thrust into my face. I lay there without moving as a previously undiscovered hole opened in front of me, and a lascivious voice begged, 'You penetrate me now.'

I was so surprised I couldn't do a thing. Cristian turned round to face me and apologized.

'Male hormones sometimes make swine out of those who aren't really animals.'

I found myself remembering what Felipe had been telling me, and thinking this was some kind of bad joke.

6th June 1997

Bidugi is going round and round the flat, exploring her new home. Granny has died. She suffered a heart attack, and at her age there was no way to save her. I feel as though I have lost a part of myself, just when we were beginning to have a great relationship. And she never got the card I sent her from Peru. Life seems very unfair to me at the moment, and I could not think of what I had done to deserve such a hard time. Death is terrible not so much for those who go through it, but for those left behind.

10th July 1997

'They're all useless in your office!' Hassan shouted over the phone, as if there was interference and he was calling from China. 'A young lady who must have been on work experience insisted there was no Val working there.'

I had forgotten how authoritarian Hassan could be. He wants to have everything at once, like a spoilt child. That's why he's still in touch with me. Basically, I gave him all that he wants from a woman: sex, youth and no questions asked.

When I first met him, I immediately felt a lot of respect and tenderness for him, as well as sexual curiosity to experiment with a much older man. He was sitting on a sofa in the Hyatt hotel bar, while I was dining with a client in the restaurant. I was uncomfortable because I kept having to avoid the ogling of Luca, the Italian chef, who seemed to have taken a liking to me. Luca looked like a drug-addicted sailor who had just got out of jail. His arms were covered in tattoos with the names of all the women he had been with. Every night after he had finished work he would come up to my bedroom door and beg me to let him in, or send me poems written in a bastard French full of spelling mistakes, which he must have learnt from his Gallic cellmates. I could not stand him.

That night, Hassan was quick to understand what was going on and came to my rescue by inviting me to have a drink with him. In those days he went around like a government minister, and wore extremely elegant Yves Saint Laurent suits. He had about half the hotel staff in his pocket. Every time a waiter came by they would bow to him or greet him as though he owned the entire country. I was on cloud nine with him beside me, and it was then I understood what the phrase 'power is an aphrodisiac' means. I wanted to try out something that drives a lot of women crazy: being with a rich and powerful man. His looks are nothing to write home about, but that to me is not the important thing. I fell for Hassan straight away, because he has a lantern jaw just like Klaus Kinski, and that little physical detail was enough to make him charismatic. This and his natural eloquence were enough to seduce me right from the start.

I was attracted by his calm assurance, disturbed only on those occasions when he was giving orders to his subordinates, who could do nothing but obey him. It wasn't even any problem for us to go up to my room, in a country where it was forbidden for a man to accompany a woman upstairs if she was not married. In fact, our relationship had started one night when he had hidden in my bedroom with a huge bunch of roses to offer me. He had overcome all kinds of obstacles to be with me, and he was taking giant strides towards becoming subconsciously dependent on me.

'Well, Hassan, I'm surprised that they didn't explain

what happened. I was sacked last April,' I told him brusquely, annoyed at the way he had spoken and by the fact of being unemployed.

'What did you do to make them throw you out so suddenly?' he barked.

'Nothing at all,' I said, hurt and upset. 'They were laying people off, and I happened to be the first in line. What are you suggesting? That I set it up to give myself problems, just when my life was more or less organized and peaceful?'

Hassan, who is always so proud of being a liberal, Western-educated Moslem, will not admit it, but being a woman is a problem in itself.

'OK, calm down!' he said, his voice softening as he realized he had no reason to be on his high horse with me. 'What do you intend to do?'

There was genuine warmth in his voice as he asked this, and I could tell he had something in mind.

'Look for work, what else?'

'Why don't you come to Morocco for a few days, and we can talk it over? I need a French-speaking woman like you on my newspaper. And you can have a bit of a break from that crazy European life you lead.'

The thought that Hassan might be able to help me professionally both attracted and repelled me, so in the end I said I wouldn't go to Morocco, even though I was thoroughly fed up with being at home at a loose end. It was suddenly being inactive rather than any economic pressure that most upset me, because during the years I worked for Andres I earned enough to have saved quite a tidy sum, sufficient to allow me to live comfortably without having to worry for a reasonably long period.

I have always been more of an ant than a grasshopper.

'Think it over.'

'I will, Hassan, and thanks.'

'You don't have to thank me,' he said, before ending the conversation.

We both put the phone down at the same time.

25th July 1997

It was eleven at night, and I was the first to arrive at the bar where I had arranged to meet Sonia for a drink. When she arrived fifteen minutes late, she floated into the bar with her hair flowing loose around her, and her small body apparently weightless. Sonia walks as gracefully as a classical ballet dancer.

'Things have got so bad I'm thinking of advertising for a boyfriend,' she told me, in tears.

'You, an advert? Isn't that going a bit far, Sonia? Don't tell me you can't find a man without the classified ads. If you were sixty and still single I might understand it, but not at your age!'

'I don't expect you to understand. But I have to say I'm on the point of throwing in the towel. I'm really depressed again. I have irregular heartbeats and I can't sleep at night.'

'Oh come on, having a boyfriend isn't everything. It'll happen – but only if you stop obsessing about it. And besides, you never go out. How do you expect to find your soulmate if you're never around?'

'I know, but I've never liked to go out hunting for a boyfriend.'

'I'm not saying that's what you should do; simply go out and have a good time, that's all.'

'But the way I look, no one's even going to notice me.'

'Didn't you just tell me you weren't looking for anyone? Come on, Sonia, snap out of it. I can't bear you to be like this when we meet.'

'Anyway, I hate one-night stands,' Sonia went on.

'Who's talking about that? You can sleep with the same guy several nights running, if that's what you want.'

'Now you're deliberately misunderstanding me. I can't imagine sex without love.'

'Oh Jesus, there you go again! I reckon you have to give things a try before you can fall in love. Don't be so prejudiced, and don't feel guilty if you like someone and sleep with them the first time you meet.'

Sonia and I have very different ideas about sex and love. In fact, I don't really know what it means to fall in love, and it doesn't really bother me that much. I consider it a privilege to be able to follow my animal instincts and enjoy myself exactly as I please, without getting involved. I tried explaining this to Sonia, but she shook her head the whole time. She said she couldn't do it, because she was brought up the old-fashioned way.

'I was, too,' I told her, trying to make her see that this had nothing to do with it. But her suggestion about placing an advert had stayed in my mind, and given me an idea.

'OK, let's drop it. The adverts thing is nonsense, I know,' she said, draining her glass.

I accompanied her home, and managed to leave her in a more positive frame of mind. She drifted up the stairs like a shadow, lighter than a cotton ball. And I knew what I was going to do: in September, I would put an advert in the paper looking for work. If Mohammed won't go to the mountain, the mountain must come to Mohammed.

The Cop

In the afternoon, Cristian called. He wanted to tell me he had a girlfriend.

'What's the big deal? I'm not jealous.'

There was such a profound silence after my relaxed response that I even wondered if he was still there.

'Yes, I'm here,' he said in a low voice. 'I didn't think that was how you were going to react.'

'Why not? What would you have preferred? For me to start shouting or crying, begging you to leave your girlfriend for me?'

'Something of the sort. Nothing like the way you reacted, anyway.'

He was disappointed. We all like to feel someone is in love with us, even if we don't feel the same about them. And my reaction wasn't exactly that of a woman who was madly in love.

'Well, I'm not jealous at all. I never asked if you were free. It's your problem, not mine.'

'The thing is, I don't want to become sexually dependent on someone, and we're seeing more and more of each other. I'm in love with my girlfriend, and don't want to lose her.'

I couldn't help laughing.

'So you're in love with her, but fuck someone else.'

'Yes, I know, I know! That's why I feel bad and prefer to put a stop to our relationship. I think that deep down you scare me.'

In other words, he did not want to see me again. I understood that it was not so much me he was scared of, but his own impulses. He did not want to face up to what he really was, so after his little peccadillo with me, he decided not to risk any further adventures.

I respect his decision. What I did not like was his way of conveying it to me. Doing it over the phone was a real coward's way out.

30th July 1997

I was not too bothered about Cristian, because I had my eye on a policeman who was on guard outside the station near my place. He has already offered me his broadest smile, and every time I go past I can see him staring at me. He looks so elegant in his uniform, particularly the way his shirt buttons are tight round his neck because it's too small for him. I think he likes me because I arouse something in him. The cop, who says his name is Toni, is shorter than me, and has cropped black hair. He always stands there very erect, and what I can see of his chest under the uniform appears to promise a powerful, muscular body. Toni's only visible sign of weakness is a funny big freckle that he has just above his right upper lip.

When I gave him my phone number, the cop's freckle bobbed upwards as his mouth lifted in a sincere smile.

8th August 1997

Tonight I took the cop to bed with me. We spent the whole night together, and made love several times, in Toni's tiny room that has no furniture apart from a lovely rug where he keeps his weights. From time to time he closed his eyes to avoid witnessing the sins he was committing, and drew the covers up over his face. At about five in the morning, I was awakened by the sound of water from the bathroom. I turned over in bed, and when I found I was all alone I realized there was a light on in the bathroom, and made out Toni's shadow under the door. I did not move. He emerged, trying not to make any noise, and as he slipped back into bed beside me I suddenly noticed the smell of the sperm all over the sheets. The persistent smell that I had tasted with the tip of my tongue. I was overcome by a sudden sense of shame which made me dive down under the covers, and when I woke up later that morning I found I was at the bottom of the bed, rolled up like a sausage.

10th September 1997

I spent the entire summer with Toni, but our fun came to an end when they transferred him to Malaga. He had put in a request several months earlier because his family is from Andalucia, and it was finally accepted. I'm very pleased for his sake. Thanks to an advert I placed, I have got a rather boring job as a freelance translator, which allows me to survive without touching my savings. It's better than nothing, but I'd like to find something else. I'm starting to feel restless.

The Argument

As I was leaving my flat today, I ran into Felipe, who was arriving at his office on a motorbike. I was happy to see him, as we hadn't bumped into each other for a long while. I must admit I no longer saw what had attracted me to him the first time we met. When I ran into him again, he was just a shy, unremarkable young man.

'Hello there!' he said, parking his bike. 'It's been a long time!'

'Hi there Felipe! Yes, I've been rather busy. How are things?'

'Could be better. I'm preparing a press pack to send to foreign magazines. Trying to drum up publicity. I've even had a call from one in South Africa.'

'Wow! You're going to be really famous.'

'All I want is for the company to be successful.'

'I'm sure it'll work out. You'll see.'

'Do you think so?' He didn't seem very sure.

'Of course. And if you need any help, don't be afraid to ask. Who knows, I might be useful.'

'Of course, of course! Thanks anyway,' he said.

We said goodbye, and he went off with his helmet under his arm. While I was trying to cross the road, he suddenly shouted at me.

'Hey, Val! You speak several languages, don't you?'

'Yes, why?'

'Can you speak English?'

'Yes, quite well.'

'I'd like you to help me with my publicity. I have to write it in English, and I don't know very much. Would you mind having a look at it when you have time?'

'Of course not, count on me. I'll call in at your office, OK?'

'Fine. And thanks again.'

I crossed the street.

25th September 1997

I stopped by at Felipe's office to look at his publicity pack. The English was so bad it needed redoing from scratch, and I told him so.

'You'll have to start again. I can do it, with your help. You can't send it out as it is. It's full of grammatical errors and spelling mistakes.'

Felipe was downcast, especially as I didn't beat about the bush when I told him how awful it was.

Eventually, after Felipe asked me who I took him for, I stormed out. We had such a bad argument I swore to myself I would never get in touch with that asshole ever again.

In the evening, Sonia rang to tell me she had found her soulmate: a handsome twenty-three-year-old musician she had met completely by chance. In the metro, as she was leaving work. He dropped his violin at her feet, and she helped him pick it up. They started talking about music, and he gave her some free tickets for a concert he was giving.

'See? I told you that you would find someone when you least expected it. The trick is not to be looking desperately for someone to come along. If you go around like a crazy woman begging a man to fall in love with you, they all run off in the opposite direction.'

She agreed with me. But now I have no lover and I've lost my friend too, because she wants to spend all her time with her lovey-dovey. And I'm condemned to be the wise woman who has to rely on casual encounters.

Sleeping With The Enemy

Some loves can be lethal . . .

The worst thing that can happen in life is to find you have your fiercest enemy in your home with you, without you realizing it.

I came to see that deep down I was bored with my hectic sexual life, leaping from one bed to the next and then suddenly finding myself all alone. It wasn't that I was desperate to meet the love of my life and change overnight, but I wanted to find someone special who could make me feel alive, and who would feel the same way about me. I was beginning to think Sonia was right, and that my moment had come too.

When Granny died, I went back to France for the funeral and to collect the few things she had left me: a calendar she had hung in the bathroom ever since she had bought it in the Fifties, and the cat Bigudi, which no one else wanted because she was antisocial and did not get on either with people or with other animals.

Bigudi more or less adopted me: I was the only person

who could get close without her growling in a way that sounded more like a dog than a cat.

Then one fateful day I fell in love.

I'll remember that moment all my life. Jaime was built like Imanol Arias. He was tall and thin, with prominent cheekbones and a big nose that had a tiny mole right on its tip. Rather than embarrassing him, this blemish gave him an excuse to make it the main topic of conversation whenever anyone mentioned it.

But when we first met, it was his hands that caught my attention. They were as long and fine as a virtuoso pianist's. He was laid-back, with an air of mystery about him, and a way of talking that made both men and women fall enchanted at his feet. In fact, he would boast that he could get any woman he wanted to, and it was when I saw how similar we were in that respect that I fell in love with him. At first I thought Jaime was someone who had been sent my way by Felipe. But eventually I concluded that however much Felipe and I had argued, he could not have been so cruel and vindictive or so vengeful as to create a character as vile and Machiavellian as Jaime.

Jaime was nothing more than a resentful loser, a piece of human trash. He had never managed to fulfil his dream of being a successful entrepreneur, so instead he gradually invented another personality for himself. I must say, I could never understand why he had not succeeded, because he seemed to be brilliant and to have everything going for him: he was a trained economist and had a lengthy and impressive CV. It must have been that in his case the forces of evil were just too much for the good that every human being possesses somewhere inside them. So Jaime used his power to destroy everything around him, and in particular anyone who was successful. He could never allow anyone to enjoy the success that eluded him.

The first time I slept with Jaime, I discovered he had a big patch of dead skin on his right heel, which he scraped off with a scalpel to prevent it affecting his walk. The patch was a bright purple colour that frightened me when I first saw it. This blemish, like the mole on his nose, only served to increase his mystery, and to make this monster more attractive. He had the gift of turning what might have repelled other people into something that attracted them.

There were no two ways about it, it was love at first sight. At least for me it was. For him, it was nothing more than a game, which he had decided to play to the bitter end.

The Interview

I received several replies to the advert I placed looking for work, but none of them seemed interesting enough to get in touch with and arrange to meet. Then one day I got a letter from someone called Jaime Rijas, a business consultant, who needed an office manager. In the letter he gave a mobile phone number to ring to arrange an interview. The first time I called I had no luck. His mobile was permanently switched off. When I did finally manage to get through, the person who answered gave me a very good impression. He sounded very professional and was looking for someone equally serious to work for him. We agreed to meet at his office after lunch.

6th May 1998

Jaime's offices were in the heart of Barcelona, in the Eixample district, in a pale pink building with wide balconies. When I arrived at the agreed time, the door was opened by a man of around fifty, with a lively look in his eye and smoking a pipe. I thought the secretaries must still be at lunch, which meant that this gentleman, who looked more like an executive than an administrative assistant, had been obliged to answer the door himself. We exchanged a few words and then Jaime appeared, limping slightly, from his room at the far end of the corridor. The man with the pipe disappeared almost at once, while Jaime shook my hand vigorously.

'Is there something wrong with your leg?' I asked him, trying to be friendly.

'No, it's nothing. I pulled a muscle playing tennis last weekend,' he replied, in a very cold tone that suggested it was not worth talking about.

He immediately ushered me into his office. It was a rather dark room that gave onto the interior courtyard of the building. He switched on a halogen lamp, and I was surprised to see so little furniture in the office for someone who was supposed to be a company director. For a second time Jaime, who was observing the way I was taking everything in, stressed how unimportant it was.

'Don't pay any attention to the way the office looks. We are in the process of moving in. Everything still has to arrive,' he explained.

The room must have been four metres wide, and the only furniture was a stupendously big President desk, and a black leather chair with wheels. There were two or three books on labour legislation on the desk, and little else. The interview began.

'I am Jaime Rijas, partner and director general of this company. The person who showed you in was the other partner, Joaquin Blanco. We're looking for a trustworthy person to organize this office and to build up a good relationship with our clients. In other words, a kind of public relations person. Did you bring your CV?'

Jaime spoke with all the seriousness and solemn air of a university professor. I could see he was someone who commanded respect. He did not seem to be easily approachable.

I handed him my CV, and he began to read it in silence. When he looked up, I felt even more intimidated.

'I hope the references you supply here are proper ones, because I always telephone to make sure. Do you have any problem with my calling your previous employers to check what they think of your work?'

'No, sir, on the contrary,' I answered, confident I had nothing to be ashamed of.

'Why did you leave your last job?'

'Because I was fired. I'm not sure if that's the best way to put it, but they were cutting down on staff, and I was the first to go, Mr . . .'

'Rijas.'

'I'm sorry?'

'Jaime Rijas,' he said, rummaging in a drawer until he found a business card to give me. 'Well anyway, I'll ring them.'

'You can speak to Mr Andres Martinez. He used to be my boss.'

'Fine.' He wrote the name at the bottom of my CV. 'Obviously,' he went on, 'I have to tell you that you're not the only candidate for the job. I've already seen quite a few, and there are three more after you. You will understand how important it is I make the right choice.'

'I understand, but I'm not sure I did the right thing in

coming to the interview. To be frank, I don't know whether the position would suit me. Until now I've always worked in publicity. I would have to think it over. What sort of salary are you offering?'

'About two hundred and fifty thousand pesetas a month, before deductions.'

'To tell you the truth, Mr Rijas, that is not exactly the best offer I've ever had.'

'That's what we would be prepared to pay during the probationary months; when we sign the proper contract we would reconsider. And of course that does not include expenses and a small commission we would pay if your public relations efforts helped lead to any new contract.'

'I understand, and thank you for seeing me and considering me for the position.'

'May I ask you another question?'

He sat up in his chair and peered at me far more seriously than at the start of the interview.

'Yes, of course.'

'Are you married?'

This did not come as much of a surprise. A lot of employers ask the same question.

'No, sir. I'm not married, and I have no children.'

'A boyfriend?'

He sat staring me in the face so intently I was flustered.

'I don't think that is a relevant question, Mr Rijas,' I said, angrily.

He did not seem upset by the way I reacted. On the contrary, he immediately became more concerned.

'I know it might seem an odd question. But I need

someone with no family commitments. It's likely that whoever gets the job will have to travel quite frequently. That's why I need a woman who has no emotional ties.'

I didn't find this explanation very convincing, but I answered all the same.

'I understand. In my case, I have neither family nor emotional ties.'

'Good. That's all I wanted to know.'

After that our conversation became a little more relaxed. We talked about the time I had spent in Spain, why I had left France, and the possibilities of promotion within the company. The end of the interview was very friendly, and when we shook hands to say goodbye he promised to call me within a week to tell me what decision he had reached, after carrying out all the other interviews.

I wasn't completely sure it was the sort of job I wanted, but then again, I wasn't losing anything by going for it. I had formed contradictory impressions of Jaime. On the one hand he had seemed very professional and serious, but on the other his prying questions into my personal life had left me nonplussed. I found the mixture of solemnity and shamelessness very seductive. Above all, Jaime was a great psychologist of women.

14th May 1998

After thinking it over carefully, I've decided not to accept the job offer from Mr Rijas, should he call me to say that I have been chosen. The position is not at all what I am looking for, so I want to go on with my search – and anyway, I'm pretty certain he won't call me again.

113

But I was wrong. This morning his secretary rang to tell me I had been shortlisted, and invited me to call at the office again in the afternoon to speak to Jaime.

Without much enthusiasm, I turned up at the office more out of a sense of professional duty and so as not to upset them, than because I wanted to work there.

Jaime Rijas was much more relaxed and friendly than the first time. I was surprised at how certain he seemed that I would accept the offer.

'It's a very prestigious post. I have chosen you and another young lady, who has just graduated from the Barcelona Business School. If you are the one who finally gets the job, it will mean you discover all the secrets of a lot of companies, and will come to understand what makes them a success or a failure. Our consultancy is about helping them meet proper business standards, amongst other things. It's fascinating!'

'I don't doubt it, Mr Rijas. I'm not saying the job isn't interesting, simply that it may not be what I am looking for. I think someone with a business diploma might be more suited for this kind of consultancy than I am.'

There I was, busily doing myself down. But Jaime insisted on trying to convince me it was exactly the job I was looking for.

'Between you and me, diplomas aren't worth much. What I appreciate are people and their potential.'

'Yes, I completely agree.'

'So we're beginning to see eye to eye,' he said, smiling. 'Perhaps if I offered you more money, you might be tempted to accept?'

'I'm not sure. It's not just the money.'

'Think it over. It's also a question of your career.'

'I will.'

We said goodbye, and he promised to call me within a couple of days.

The Trap

16th May 1998

Despite my lack of interest in the job, there is no doubt that Mr Rijas exerts a fascination over me that I find hard to understand. I liked his appearance, but I was even more taken by his manner, the self-confidence he displayed that made him seem indestructible, and his lack of fear when faced with challenges. I thought that his determination grew when confronted with a blunt 'no'. He took rejection personally, and was happy if he could change it to a committed 'yes'. That is what makes him tick. I was a 'no' from start to finish, and he was determined to get me to change at any cost, by any means whatsoever.

Today he called me as promised. But his conversation went off in a completely non-professional direction.

'My partner and I have reached our decision. But there's a problem, which I'd like to discuss with you personally.'

'What sort of problem?' I asked, my curiosity aroused,

even though I was pretty sure I wouldn't be of any help.

Jaime adopted the tone of someone taking me into his confidence, even though he still hadn't explained what all this was about.

'I think you're someone I can talk openly to. But I need to see you for that. Do you mind if we just meet and talk?'

It all seemed very odd to me, but I agreed. I suppose that deep down I wanted to see him again. I still don't understand how I allowed myself to be caught in that spider's web which any outside observer could have seen would be fatal. I have always had a headstrong nature, and like challenges.

'How about if I pick you up tomorrow evening around seven?'

'Wouldn't it be better to meet in your office?' I asked, not liking the personal twist all this was taking.

'I would prefer not to. I need a more neutral space to put the matter to you. Things are too busy here: consultants are coming in and out the whole time. I'm always being asked to do things. All the usual business stuff. That's why I prefer somewhere quieter. I'll take you for a drink – without any ulterior motives, of course.'

'OK, that's fine.'

I couldn't help wondering why he had mentioned ulterior motives. He knew my address from my CV, so we agreed to meet outside my place at seven the next evening.

17th May 1998

I got in his car and we started touring the centre of

117

Barcelona looking for somewhere to park. I had not said much up to then, but had listened to him talking about what had happened during the day, and how much his company stood to make that month. According to him, the business was a huge success; he was so full of enthusiasm I began to wonder what kind of problem a man like him that everything seemed to shine on could possibly have. He suggested we went down to Maremagnum, where we could park easily and without the threat of being towed away. I agreed.

We went up to the top floor of the shopping centre, which is open to the skies, and where there are an incredible number of bars trying to attract customers from the crowds that could easily fill a football stadium. After a short wait, we found two seats on a terrace next to a mini-golf. We ordered two gin and tonics.

'What did you have to tell me that was so important, and why have you brought me to a place like this?'

I could tell Jaime was rather taken aback by my audacity, but he rushed to reassure me.

'First of all, why don't you call me Jaime? And don't stand on ceremony with me.'

I nodded in agreement. If he was going to confide in me, we should be on first-name terms, and besides, he had asked me so politely!

'OK. Well then, I'm an economist, I'm forty-nine and I've always been a businessman. I have very clear ideas about what I should and should not do. In all those years, this is the first time something like this has happened to me, so I thought it would make sense to talk it over with someone who would come to it without preconceived ideas – and that's why I wanted to talk to you.'

'Me?' I exclaimed, pouring more tonic into my gin.

It was a surprisingly cold night, and as he spoke Jaime rubbed his hands to warm up. His gestures were so florid it was as though he were about to speak to some huge public meeting.

'Yes, you!' he said, pointing a finger at my heart.

'Why me? We have only met for a job interview; we don't know each other at all. What makes you think I'm the right person to give you advice?'

'Precisely because we don't know each other. That means your opinion will be all the more objective. Something tells me your advice could be very helpful. Don't ask me to explain why, because I couldn't. But I'm convinced you can help me.'

'Fine, but that depends on what the problem is. How am I supposed to help?' I asked him again, running out of patience.

Jaime was so calm he didn't seem as if anything could worry him, but he replied, 'I've met someone at work, but given the fact that I run the company, I'm not sure how I should behave towards her. In the past I've always been able to control my impulses, especially in a work context. Above all, it's a question of ethics. That's what I've always thought. But now the situation is getting beyond me, and I don't know what to do.'

'So how can I help?'

I still didn't have the faintest idea what this man wanted from me. He took his time, sipping his drink, and then putting it back on the table and playing with the cocktail stick.

'What would you advise?'

'How should I know? Who is this person? Does she work for your company?'

'No, but I'm in contact with her indirectly. I don't know her very well. She works for someone else. But the worst of it is I've fallen head over heels in love with her.'

'Does she know?'

'I think she's an intelligent woman, and she must have realized there's something going on. But so far she hasn't made any comment, and I haven't said anything about how I feel. But these things are bound to show, aren't they? I reckon that deep down she doesn't want to face reality, because she's afraid to.'

'Well, if you really want my opinion, I think the first thing you should do is talk to her. Perhaps she hasn't even realized how you feel.'

'No, I think she knows perfectly well what's going on. But it's a very delicate situation. How would you react, if you were her?'

'Well, if I were in that situation and I liked the man, I wouldn't give it a second thought. It depends on the work relationship you two have. I find it hard to be completely sincere with you. Not everyone would take risks like I do.'

'Aha, thanks for your honesty, anyway.'

He seemed truly grateful.

'Why don't you talk to her?'

'I've tried, but I can't find the words, so whenever I come to the crucial moment I start to talk about work instead.'

'What are you afraid of?'

'Her telling me she doesn't feel the same about me.'

I was surprised at this unguarded reply. On the few

occasions I had met him, Jaime had always given the impression of being in control and of being very sure of himself. Now it seemed that wasn't true at all.

'But if you don't talk openly to her, you'll never get anywhere. Things will stay stuck where they are now.'

'You're right, and that's why I wanted to talk to you. I knew your opinion would help a lot.'

I must admit, I was pleased he had turned to me. All women like that. But I still did not understand why he had such confidence in me.

'Well, how about going to have something to eat? I'm hungry, and since we're talking like this, why not do it at a proper table? I know a restaurant near here where you can get really fresh seafood.'

This sounded like the kind of invitation a friend might make, so I again said yes. What Jaime was trying to do was to make me drop my guard so that we could be more friendly; when I had seen him at his office I had always been very distant.

He paid for the drinks and we walked to the restaurant, which was about five hundred metres away towards the Olympic Village. The owner, who appeared to know Jaime well, greeted him warmly and quickly found us a table although the place looked full. He offered us an aperitif, and Jaime asked me if it was all right for him to order seafood platters for both of us.

'A nice plate of seafood to cheer us up, don't you think?'

I love seafood, so I was all for it. It seemed we had similar tastes. He ordered a bottle of the best champagne, and proposed a toast to friendship. It seemed more like he was trying to impress and seduce me. For a while we just chatted, and then he started again with more personal questions.

'Were you really annoyed the other day when I asked if you had a boyfriend?'

'I was a bit shocked,' I said frankly. 'I could understand why you asked whether I was married or not. But why should it matter about a boyfriend?'

'It was very important for me to know.'

'I know. You told me you wanted the person you took on to be free. If that is what you're looking for, I think you're going to find it difficult.'

'Well, that wasn't the real reason.'

I put my fork down.

'Ah, no? Why was it then?'

'It was to find out whether I could ask you out tonight,' replied Jaime, going on eating. 'If you'd said you had a boyfriend, I'd have tried another tack.'

'What?'

I was left speechless, unable to react.

'Yes. If you did have a boyfriend, I would have pursued you anyway.'

By this time we had drunk quite a lot, so I thought it was the drink talking. I suddenly felt uncomfortable, and could not help laughing nervously.

'You wouldn't have been put off by my having a boyfriend?'

'On the contrary, I would have done all I could to get you to leave him,' he said, as self-assured as he had been at our first meeting.

'What are you talking about?' I said, still laughing nervously. 'Haven't you just been telling me you're in love with another woman?'

I couldn't understand a thing, and thought he must be completely crazy.

'Yes, it's true, I am in love with a woman.'

'So I see,' I said sarcastically. 'You're in love, but that doesn't stop you trying to pick me up.'

He burst out laughing.

'How silly can you be?' he said affectionately. 'You don't get it, do you?'

'No, the truth is I don't understand you. You're like all men. You have a woman you're in love with, yet you can't take your eyes off the others. I really don't get it.'

I no longer cared what he thought of me. I had decided that after this conversation I never wanted to see him again in my life. He was obviously a dangerous self-obsessed fool. All of a sudden, Jaime stopped laughing and called the waiter over. He asked for another bottle of champagne, then did not say another word until our glasses were filled again. He raised his and said, 'Here's to you, Val, the woman who is driving me crazy.'

He stared at my glass, expecting me to raise it too, but I was so dumbfounded I couldn't even move. What he had said was the last thing I had expected, and no one could have been more surprised. He asked me again to drink with him, and in the end I raised my glass like a zombie.

'That's what I wanted to tell you. That's why I asked you to have dinner with me. I'm crazy about you,' he said, craning his neck towards me across the table. 'You're the woman I'm in love with.'

I sat there open-mouthed, while he downed his entire glass. I couldn't swallow a sip of mine.

'Phew! I'm glad that's over,' he said, obviously relieved. 'Now I've got it off my chest. I just had to talk to you.'

I still couldn't believe my ears, but just sat there staring at the champagne bubbles rising to the surface in my glass.

All of a sudden Jaime looked sad, and then he said, 'I'm so sorry. I didn't mean to upset you. I'm really sorry.'

He asked for the bill. I still felt very strange: I'm not used to someone I hardly know declaring his love for me. He paid and we left in silence.

'I'll take you home. I hope you don't mind. When I go out with someone, I like to see them safely home.'

My head was starting to ache. I had drunk too much, and had no idea what to say to him. I decided to let him have it his way. When we reached my building, I was surprised again when he said good night and left at once. But I did nothing to stop him, because I was still stunned by his sudden declaration, and needed some time to take it in and recover.

20th June 1998

Almost a month has gone by since we started going out together. After his declaration, Jaime did not call again except once to tell me that if I wanted it, the job was mine, whether or not I was interested in him romantically. I turned the offer down: it was clear after the dinner that I couldn't work in his firm, and that I would have to look for something else, because I had decided to go out with him. It was either one thing or the other. I have to admit I was impressed by the way he had taken the plunge and declared his love for me; but I was equally impressed by the discretion he had shown afterwards. He seemed to have understood perfectly that I didn't want to be pressured, and in so doing he was creating just the right kind of climate for me to fall in love with him. He had also seen from the start that I was not interested in the job. He must have thought I was a very self-possessed woman with very definite views, someone who can only respond if she doesn't feel too hassled. In fact, I'm the perfect prey for any daring hunter.

Since then we've seen each other on several occasions, during which he has taken it for granted that I'm eventually bound to fall into his arms. He wants me to understand quite clearly that he is very sure of himself in that respect, and that sooner or later it will happen. I am starting to like him more and more, but I haven't been to bed with him yet, as I usually do. This time I prefer to wait.

We agreed to meet today just to talk. Jaime said he wanted to tell me all about his life, because he didn't want to have any secrets from me. He told me the story of his marriage to his ex-wife, who now has breast cancer, and confessed that he had really loved her, but could never manage to stay faithful, and one day she had had enough and left him.

He wanted to show me his weak points one by one, like someone going through a manual. That was also part of his elaborate strategy. And the way he told the story meant I could not stay unaffected. He still spoke with great authority, but it was as if he was very sorry for what he had done. I could feel myself being gradually seduced by his personality – by his failings above all, by the way he treated his women, all mixed together with an unconsciously paternal attitude. He told me that for seven years he had been in a relationship with an ex-model, Carolina. He said his passion for her had known no bounds, and that this relationship too had come to an end because he was unfaithful with another woman – who turned out to be none other than Carolina's best friend. I soon realized the message he was trying to convey with every word he spoke: will you be the woman who can tame me? That was how he lured me: now he is a challenge for me.

He also talked a lot about his two children, whom he only sees at weekends. I found his pride at being a father very touching. I suppose this was because it was a facet of his character I had not known until now, and also because as I approached thirty my female hormones were pushing me towards being a mother.

25th June 1998

Today I made love to Jaime for the first time since I met him. He came to my flat, which I welcomed him into with open arms, and we made love on the kitchen table. There was nothing out of this world about it. He seemed very tired, and I can understand that however much we'd like to be, we're not always a hundred per cent. I must admit though I was rather disappointed. I thought it would be much more romantic. It only took five minutes, and for four of them I was trying to convince him to use a contraceptive.

'Do you think a man of my age uses a condom? It's total crap!'

In the end, he gave in. But I know it didn't exactly please him.

Our Love Nest

3rd July 1998

In these first months of our relationship, Jaime is behaving like a perfect gentleman. Everything is going marvellously. Yet just occasionally, I can see and detect some odd things. Perhaps it's only my imagination. I have never interfered in anyone else's life before, but now I find myself looking into his diary, and feeling terribly guilty about it. I found coded entries, a sign that he is hiding something from me, but as yet I have no proof. In the end I chose not to worry too much about it, and we have gone on seeing each other. Then today at noon he asked me to go and live with him.

15th July 1998

We have to find somewhere to live together. We have already agreed on the district we would like: Barcelona's Olympic Village, mainly because you can see the sea from there. Both of us adore the sea. I've always dreamed of living in a huge loft facing the sea and the beach, and now at last with Jaime this can become a reality. With some difficulty we eventually found a flat of a hundred and twenty square metres looking onto the beach, with private parking and round-the-clock security. I insisted the flat should have at least three bedrooms, so that we can have his children to stay. When I explained why I wanted so many rooms, Jaime was in complete agreement, but I was surprised that the idea didn't come from him. I think that he probably wants to cement our relationship before he mixes it with his family.

This morning we went to sign the rental agreement at a very demanding estate agency. Jaime had to bring half a million pesetas in cash to cover the deposit and the first rent payment. I went with him because we had said we would put the agreement in both our names; I thought this was clear, but then at the last minute Jaime asked if I had a problem with using just my name.

'I thought we were both going to be on it. Is there something wrong?'

'No, don't worry. I'll pay the rent, but if it's all the same to you, I'd prefer not to have my name on the contract. I don't want my ex-wife to find out. If she did, she'd only ask me to pay more for the kids.'

At that moment, I picked up on an important detail. The kids, as he calls them, are adults, and each of them lives with their own partner, works, and is completely independent. The payments for them must have been agreed more than ten years ago, so his explanation did not really stand up.

However, I was so excited at the idea of living with him in this fantastic apartment I did not want to cause any problems, so I accepted that only my name should be on the rental agreement.

We told the agency all this, and that although I did not have steady employment, I had more than enough money to pay up to two years' rent. The agency said that the owner did not wish to rent to anyone without a fixed job. I was devastated, because I could see our dream home slipping away from us.

Yet again, Jaime said he would deal with everything, and this afternoon we went back to the agency, he gave them some papers, and I signed the contract. As we were leaving, I said how surprised I was that everything had been sorted out, and Jaime told me that he had showed them my bank statements and that had been sufficient. It was only later that I found out he had given them my latest 'payslip', which he had drawn up in his office without saying a word to me, signing it with his name and putting his company stamp on it.

20th July 1998

I feel happy because this morning we moved in. We did it all in a few hours, as I have so few things. Jaime only brought clothing from his mother's house, where he stays, and some paintings which he says were left him by his father from his private collection, and which are extremely valuable. It's not much for such a huge flat, and I can see we're going to need lots of furniture.

This afternoon we went on a tour of all the local furniture shops. When we had chosen what we wanted, Jaime insisted on paying for it all despite my protests, because I wanted to share the expense.

25th and 26th July 1998

Jaime has told me he has a chalet outside Madrid, and that he often meets up with his children there at weekends. I was delighted at the idea of spending my weekends there too, but he said he would first have to explain to them that he now had a serious relationship with someone. But I would need to be patient because his son, although he is almost the same age as me, gets very jealous when he sees his father with women who are not his mother. I could understand that, and told myself I would just have to be patient and understanding. Above all, I wanted them to accept me. After all, I'm going to be the stepmother of a boy and girl who are already grown-up.

As today is Friday, Jaime caught the shuttle to Madrid to meet his children. He called me soon afterwards to find out how I was, and our conversation on the phone was very affectionate. We seem to have a marvellous and happy future ahead of us. Curiously, now we are living together, we will probably see less of each other than when we lived apart.

I only see Sonia occasionally. She knows about my relationship with Jaime, but thinks I rushed into living with him.

'You hardly know him! And besides, he doesn't even spend a single weekend with you. Doesn't that seem odd?'

'Listen who's talking!' I said ironically. 'You were always looking for your Prince Charming, and now you're saying I rushed into it when I met mine!'

'That's not what I'm saying, Val! I'm simply

suggesting you were being a bit hasty in leaving your flat and going to live with a man you don't know at all well. Has he introduced you to his family at least?'

'Not yet, Sonia. He needs time. You can understand that, can't you? He has two children and an ex-wife who has cancer. With that situation in the family, just think what would have happened if I turned up out of the blue. It would be adding insult to injury. I don't think it's right. Not for now at least.'

'OK! I agree. You're right, it's too soon. But don't you think it's odd that he has this luxury chalet outside Madrid, and that before he met you he lived with his mother?'

Sonia was starting to make me feel nervous. At first I put her suspicions down to the sort of jealousy all women feel when one of us gets what we have all dreamed of. It's only human.

'He bought the chalet when he was going out with Carolina, a former girlfriend he met in Madrid. That's where they lived. In those days, Jaime also had an office in the capital. Whenever he came to Barcelona, he stayed with his mother. It seems perfectly normal and logical to me. There's nothing odd or mysterious in wanting to see his mother.'

'All right, but tell me just one thing. If his children live in Barcelona, why do they all have to go to Madrid to see each other?'

I had no answer to that. I could see that Sonia was very concerned about me and the new life I had chosen. She's also a bit put out because ever since I got together with Jaime, we see less of each other.

'You're right, Sonia. But you've been with your

132

boyfriend a lot as well. Anyway, I promise to ring you more often from now on. With the apartment and the move and everything, I haven't had a moment to myself. I hope you can see that. Oh, and by the way I was thinking of organizing a small dinner party next Thursday so you could meet Jaime. What do you think?'

'Of course, I'd really like that.'

'That way you can make it up to him,' I said with a laugh.

'OK, that's great.'

'You can bring your boyfriend if you like.'

Her face fell a hundred feet.

'We broke it off last week.'

I had really put my foot in it. Now I understood why she was so suspicious of Jaime. A man had dropped her, and she was angry with all males.

'He had another girlfriend he hadn't told me about. I found out by accident and told him I had had enough.'

'I understand, sweetheart. I'm really sorry. But just because it happened to you with that bastard doesn't mean all men are the same, Sonia.'

'Don't worry. I'll get over it. By the way, Bigudi really misses you.'

Hearing that made me very sad. Above all, I would like to have Bigudi back with me, but I had been forced to leave him with Sonia because Jaime can't stand cats. So for now the poor creature would not be welcome at home.

I Find a Job

27th July 1998

When Jaime got back from his family weekend, I told him about the proposed dinner on Thursday.

'I'd love to, sweetheart, but I have to spend the whole week in Malaga with Joaquin, visiting clients. I'm leaving early tomorrow, and on Friday I'm going straight to Madrid by car.'

This plan didn't exactly thrill me, but I tried to hide my feelings.

'So we're not going to see each other until Sunday?'

'It's my work, darling. Try to understand! We've got contracts with clients in the south of Spain, and we have to see them this week. I've been putting the trip off for far too long as it is. We'll be together afterwards.'

He took me in his arms, and we settled on another date for the dinner with Sonia.

After what he had told me about his marital infidelities, that night I decided to tell him about my sporadic relationships, and how easy I had always found it to take whatever man I fancied in bed with me. I wanted to be honest with Jaime, and not to hide anything. He had already warned me that, as he put it, I had to give up any other boyfriends I had hanging around. I didn't find that difficult to accept, because I haven't had any new ones for some time now, but it was hard work convincing him. Jaime is a tremendously jealous person. He promised to be faithful to me. I am twenty-nine, and although he is twenty years older than me, we have met at the same point in our lives. We are both sick and tired of the lives we were leading. I no longer even look at anyone else. I must admit, this change has surprised even me, but I suppose it's because for the first time in my life I'm really in love, and so any sexual desire I feel for anyone apart from Jaime has vanished. I'm going to be faithful to him from start to finish, and even months afterwards, should our relationship come to an end.

At night we made love. Our lovemaking has got steadily better since we no longer use contraceptives, but Jaime has a strange way of only thinking of himself. He doesn't wait for me to get any satisfaction. Sometimes he's like an animal. But I don't care. It's not what's most important to me in our relationship. Curiously, for me sex has faded into the background.

28th July 1998

Jaime has left for Malaga with Joaquin as planned. I said my tender goodbyes, urging him to be careful on the roads. As I'm going to be completely on my own for a few days, I decided to use the time to find a new job.

I've already had several offers (my advert continues to

appear in the newspaper from time to time) and there is one that looks very promising. It was from a foreign multinational clothing company based in Barcelona. They are looking for a woman to keep them informed of all the latest trends. That would mean travelling to the most important fashion fairs all over the world, sniffing out the market, and seeing what the latest fashions are each season. It's not directly linked to advertising, but I'm really attracted to the idea of working in that area. And besides, I have no problems about travelling, especially as Jaime does so much anyway.

So I went for the interview. It was all very quick, and they told me I can start in a week. I felt very happy, because it means our income will increase significantly. I've no idea what Jaime earns (he's never mentioned it), but I can see that he lives well. He always carries lots of cash on him, never checks what he's spending or appears to worry about money in any way, not even when it comes to renting an apartment in such a high-class building. On the contrary, he always insists he wants the best. Despite all this, I want to be able to help with our household expenses.

Jaime has only called a couple of times, to tell me how busy he is. Whenever I've tried to call him, his mobile has been switched off. In order not to seem untrusting, I did not ask him for his hotel number.

30th July 1998

When Jaime got back today he looked tired and anxious. As soon as he had taken his shoes off, he shut himself in the bathroom for more than an hour. I listened intently for any noise, and when I heard nothing, I asked him through the door, 'Is anything wrong, Jaime?'

'Leave me in peace!' he snapped back.

'Is there anything I can do for you, darling? Perhaps it would do you good to talk. I don't know: is something worrying you?'

'Leave me in peace!' he repeated. 'You don't have the faintest idea of the problems I've got!'

When he came out an hour later, his eyes were all puffy, and he spent all afternoon and most of the evening chain-smoking, without saying a word to me.

When he came to bed, he didn't even touch me. Until now, whenever we have spent the night together, we've made love. This was the first time he had refused.

2nd August 1998

Jaime left early for his office. I wasn't even able to tell him I was starting my new job today, when everyone else is going on holiday. Just in case he arrived home before me, I left him a note in the kitchen explaining everything. That's exactly what happened. When I got in this evening, worried about the way he had been yesterday, I found him watching TV in the living room.

'You could have told me you were starting work today,' he said reproachfully.

'I know, Jaime, but yesterday you were impossible. You didn't want to talk, and you were so closed in on yourself it seemed you had some difficulty or other.'

'I had a problem I didn't want to talk about. What's this about work?'

I explained how I had found the job, and what it implied.

'So you're going to have to travel?'

I could tell just by looking at him that he was angry.

'Yes, occasionally.'

'On your own?'

'No, with my boss. He's American. In September we have to go to a show in Italy, and . . .'

'American? Another one who'll want to fuck you!'

This unexpected reply left me speechless. Jaime was obviously in the same mood as yesterday.

'What are you talking about?'

'You heard. He wants you to travel with him so he can fuck you. You'll see. You're still too young. You don't know how things are.'

I was astounded. It didn't seem right to me for him to judge in that way someone he had never met.

'It doesn't matter. Off you go to Italy. Travel with that asshole. But if he so much as touches you, you're to take the first plane back here, got it?'

I found myself agreeing, because I was scared that if I didn't, he might have hit me.

'Yes, of course.'

'Do you promise?'

'Of course, Jaime. I promise!'

He fell silent for five minutes, and I thought the matter was over and done with.

'What about you? You want to fuck him too, don't you?'

Yet again, I was dumbstruck. I couldn't understand why he was saying this kind of thing all of a sudden.

'No, I don't want to fuck him in the slightest,' I said, my words trailing away sadly.

This time it was me who headed for the bathroom to cry. Jaime had gone too far: all at once he looked really evil, and he was obviously spoiling for a fight. He has changed so much over the past few days, he's almost like a completely different person. In the bathroom I found a small jar I had never seen before. In it were about a hundred grams of white powder; on the label were the ingredients of a chemist's prescription. As I was picking the jar up, Jaime came up silently behind me, and put a hand on my shoulder. I was so startled I almost dropped it.

'It's powder for the wound I have on my ankle. I have it specially prepared at a chemist's. It's very expensive, so leave it where it is!'

I put the jar back on the bathroom shelf and said nothing.

Every morning, Jaime uses a kind of scalpel to scrape off the layers of dead skin on his ankle. If he didn't he wouldn't be able to put on his shoe and walk properly. He has been to see several specialists and, according to him, it's a very rare phenomenon which cannot be cured. None of them had ever seen anything like it.

Broken Dishes

6th August 1998

Today was the day for Sonia to come to dinner. Jaime stayed at home working all afternoon in a room we've put a desk in, while I prepared the food in the kitchen. I've never liked cooking much, but I've taught myself through reading about it, because Jaime likes to eat well at lunch and dinnertime. No sandwiches or snacks, he warned me from the start.

While Sonia was having an aperitif in the living room, I went to find Jaime and tell him our guest had arrived. He had locked himself in the room, as if there was a treasure in there that only he should know about.

'Are you coming for dinner, darling?' I asked gently, so as not to upset him. 'Sonia's here.'

Without opening the door, Jaime replied that he'd be with us in ten minutes, after he had taken a quick shower and changed his clothes. I went back to the living room.

'You don't look happy, Val. What's wrong? Is every-thing all right?'

I didn't want to talk to my friend about the arguments Jaime and I had been having lately. I decided to give her a very different explanation.

'It's just that I'm very tired. It's my new job. There's a lot to do, and I have to get used to it. Don't forget, I haven't worked full-time for months.'

I've lost weight recently, and Sonia insisted there must be some other reason for it.

'You've only been working a week! And you've lost four kilos! Are you sure there isn't something else you don't want to talk about?'

'Yes, I'm sure, Sonia. Don't worry.'

I put on my best smile in order to convince her. She's become a bit too curious lately, questioning everything I do. When Jaime appeared, he looked fantastic: he was fresh and really handsome. He was also on his best behaviour, and when I introduced him to Sonia I could tell from her expression that she was impressed by his good looks. Exactly as I expected.

'The famous Sonia! We meet at last!' said Jaime, kiss-ing her hand.

We women are always attracted by this outmoded habit. Sonia was in seventh heaven.

'I've wanted so much to meet you too, Jaime. I knew you had to be someone special to steal Val's heart away.'

Sonia went on looking at him, doubtless thinking he looked much younger than his age.

We spent a very pleasant evening, with Jaime being completely enchanting with both Sonia and me. There was a real sparkle in his eyes, accentuated no doubt by the bottles of wine he insisted on opening, arguing that each course needed a different one. I could see he was drinking heavily, but I said nothing because I didn't want to spoil the magic of the occasion. We talked mostly about Sonia: her life and our long friendship. Then Jaime talked a bit about himself, and how much he wanted to get married to me once his wife's cancer had been sorted out. I was surprised he said this so openly, because before then he had not even mentioned the idea.

'If all goes well, we'll get married on the 2nd of May 1999,' he told Sonia.

At the end of the evening, which in fact was quite late at night, Sonia declared she wanted to go home. She too had been drinking a lot.

'How did you get here?' asked Jaime.

'By taxi,' she replied, finishing her glass of Bailey's.

'I couldn't possibly allow as attractive a woman as you to go home by taxi at this time of night. I'll take you. I'll just put a jacket on . . . and off we go.'

I didn't see anything wrong with this idea – simply Jaime showing he was friendly to a close friend of mine. He was being nice to Sonia, but to me as well, and I liked that. Of course, Sonia's impression of him had changed completely. He had been doing his utmost to make it an unforgettable evening, and it seemed he had succeeded. Sonia looked over at me, and I smiled my agreement, so she accepted Jaime's offer.

After they left, I cleared away the plates and put them in the kitchen. I did not feel like doing the dishes so late at night. When Jaime had not reappeared after more than an hour, I decided to go to bed.

All at once I was awakened by a huge crash from the

kitchen. Startled, I rushed out of bed to see what could have fallen. All the lights were out, so I did not even look to see if Jaime was in bed. When I switched the kitchen light on, I saw all the dirty plates and glasses smashed on the worktop, and bits of food all over the floor. When I saw the mess, my first reaction was to raise a hand to my mouth to stifle a scream. The kitchen looked terrible. At the far end, in the doorway of the utility room next to the street door, stood Jaime. He had his back to me, and was smoking a cigarette as he peered out of the window.

'If you couldn't be bothered to do the dishes while I was out, don't pick up the pieces now. You can do it tomorrow: that was what you intended to do, wasn't it?' he said ironically.

I didn't dare say a word, because I could not grasp what on earth was going on.

Jaime was still facing away from me, then all of a sudden he stubbed the cigarette out on the floor with his shoe and started shouting like a madman.

'None of this would have happened if you'd washed the dishes tonight!'

The kitchen stank of alcohol. Jaime had drunk himself senseless and when he got home he had swept all the plates to the floor in a fit of madness. Now he was trying to provoke me, and I burst into tears, but instead of making him feel remorseful, this only seemed to enrage him still further.

'Don't start crying now! Your face gets all puffed up, and you look dreadful!'

That was the last straw. I couldn't bear all this madness and the way he was torturing me. I ran out of the kitchen and locked myself in the bathroom, where I could cry as much as I wanted. I was splashing my face with cold water in the sink when I heard the front door slam. It was better that way. If he hadn't left, things could have ended really nastily.

7th August 1998

When I left for work this morning, Jaime still hadn't come back. He spent the whole night elsewhere, and didn't even telephone. At the office, I felt so desperate I called Sonia.

'Hello there, sweetheart,' I said, then burst into tears before she even had time to reply.

'Val, what's wrong?'

At first I couldn't get out the words, but eventually I managed to explain what had happened.

'It's Jaime.'

'You sound awful. What's been going on?'

'Sonia, what did you do last night? When Jaime got back he was completely drunk and behaved like a madman.'

'What? I don't get it. He drove me home, we chatted outside for about five minutes, then he left. That's absolutely all. He seemed fine to me. All of us drank quite a bit last night, but he didn't look out of control. He must have gone and drunk some more to get himself into such a state. When we said good night, he was charming.'

'Yes, I know he would have been, Sonia. That's why I can't understand a thing. Something else must have happened, because he was like a wild beast. When he got back, he had changed completely. I was really afraid.

And now I don't know what to do. I'm still frightened. This is the second time he's turned violent and . . .'

'Has he lifted a hand to you?' she asked, without waiting for me to finish.

'No. It's more a verbal violence directed at me and everything else that gets in his way. He smashed all the crockery last night.'

'I don't believe it . . .'

'He did, and then he said that if I'd washed up, it wouldn't have happened. It was as though he were punishing me for it. Then he stormed out. And since then I haven't heard a thing from him.'

I decided to swallow my pride and tell Sonia everything, thinking she might be able to explain what had happened to Jaime. But when she couldn't make any sense of it either, I felt even more confused.

Throughout the day I found it hard to concentrate, and I was afraid of going home. I had left without taking anything with me, but I began seriously to consider moving to Sonia's place for a few days to take stock. My relationship with Jaime is becoming increasingly strange, and I wonder if I could ever be happy with a man like that. Something is happening to him, but I haven't the faintest idea what. And he refuses to talk about it.

I arrived home late. As soon as I opened the front door, I realized Jaime was already there, because the door was no longer double-locked. I started to tremble at the thought of what might happen.

The kitchen door is immediately to the left of the entrance, and when I stepped inside the flat, I could see it was all clean and tidy.

145

Jaime came out of the living room carrying an enormous bunch of roses. When I saw how apologetic he looked, I flung myself at him, in tears.

'I'm so sorry!' he said.

He held out the bunch of roses. I was crying because on the one hand I still had no idea what had happened, and on the other I was so pleased that he was so contrite.

'Don't worry, Jaime,' I said, still sobbing, 'I suppose you have problems and don't want to talk about them.'

'Yes, it's true I've got problems. I didn't want to mention them so as not to hurt you. But I can see you're suffering anyway, so I'm going to tell you everything.'

He took me by the hand and led me into the living room. He sat down opposite me, which gave me the feeling that something really serious must be worrying him.

'There are some things we're not proud of, and for that reason we don't want to talk about them. I thought I could sort everything out on my own, but I see now it's been affecting the way I behave.'

Then he launched into an explanation of his economic situation, which he's struggling with day by day. He said he was in debt due to Joaquin, his associate, who had borrowed money from the bank a few months earlier, and asked Jaime to be his guarantor. But some time later Joaquin had stopped paying the bank, and now they were demanding the money from Jaime. He still owed five million pesetas, and even though Jaime earns large sums of money each month, he was unable to get together that much all at once, so the bank was about to seize his chalet outside Madrid.

'They're going to take away all that I sweated blood

for. I've paid for it for years and years, and now, thanks to my partner, I'm going to lose it!'

I could not believe what I was hearing. Yet he seemed so sincere and so upset that I did not question the truth of what he was saying.

'Why did you act as Joaquin's guarantor in the first place?' I asked timidly.

'How could I refuse? Apart from being business partners, we're friends, Val. At least, that's what I thought until now. Wouldn't you do the same for Sonia? It never crossed my mind he might stop paying back the loan, and land me in this situation.'

'But why did he stop paying?'

'His marriage has been on the rocks for years. For the past few months he's been drinking a lot, and spending more and more money on women. Some days when I get to work I find him asleep on his office carpet, filthy, drunk and penniless because he's been all night in one of those clubs.'

I was beginning to understand why Jaime had behaved the way he had with me. He must have felt cornered, and his nerves had made him lash out.

'That Sunday when I came back in such a bad mood, do you remember?' I nodded, and took his hands in mine. 'It was because the people from the bank had been looking for me all the time I was in Malaga. On Friday I had to go to Madrid, and there I learnt about them seizing my possessions.'

'Is there no way to stop it?'

'Yes, of course.'

'How?'

'By paying.'

Jaime was in such despair that he began to cry like a baby. Someone who was always so elegant and proud had suddenly crumpled like a little boy. His head was in my hands, but I had no idea how to comfort him.

'And do you know what's the worst?'

'No.'

'The fact that I'm taking it out on you. I feel so threatened that I'm taking it out on the person I love most in the whole wide world!'

I stroked his cheeks, trying to dry his tears. I was really affected by what he had said. He went on, 'I work like crazy to have a good life and so that my family has everything they need. My children have all they could ask for. I'm giving my ex-wife a helping hand because she's so ill and has money problems. And now this!'

There was no way to stop the flow of his tears. I was upset and felt helpless, and yet I was glad he had finally told me the truth.

'I have a week to find the money and stop the legal process. If I don't, they'll take the house.'

We spent most of the night curled up together on the sofa, covered by a thin blanket I put over us when I saw Jaime start to shudder violently. He seemed exhausted, but I lay awake turning the problem over and over in my mind. There was no way I could let something like that happen to my partner. If I love him and am living with him, I have to share his anxieties. I could not be happy if he was in such a bad state. I have to do something. I have the money he needs. I decided to take the five million pesetas out of my account, and give them to him so that he wouldn't lose his house in Madrid.

The Seizure

12th August 1998

I didn't say anything to Jaime, but I went to the bank to get out the money he needs. I was scared of carrying so much money with me, so I made three trips. The bank manager, with whom I have always had an excellent relationship, called me into his office to ask if I wasn't satisfied with the service. He was very surprised I was withdrawing all my savings. I assured him nothing was wrong, and that I had no complaints. On the contrary. I invented an excuse by saying that something unexpected had arisen that I had to deal with straight away.

Today was Wednesday, and Jaime was even more nervous than usual. I can tell the temperature of his mood by the length of time he spends locked in the bathroom in the morning. The more nervous he is, the longer he is in there, scraping the dead skin off his ankle, and leaving the basin in a disgusting mess with all the bits of dry skin and white powder.

Jaime had to leave the next day to go to Madrid and make one last attempt to negotiate with the bank. That's what he told me. I had decided not to tell him that I was going to help him until the very last minute.

When I arrived home I found him packing his suitcase to leave the next day and spend the weekend with his children. He looked up at me sadly and said, 'This may be the last one I can spend with them.'

He fell silent for a moment, then added, 'How am I going to explain to them that their home is no longer theirs?'

'You won't have to explain a thing,' I said cheerfully. 'Look, this is for you!'

I handed him an envelope. He took it cautiously, a look of surprise on his face. When he opened it, he could not believe his eyes.

'Where did you get all this?' he asked me suspiciously.

'From my own account. There's enough for you to pay back the loan.'

'Are you crazy? How on earth did you think I was going to accept it? Did you ask for a loan or something from your bank?'

'No, don't worry. I didn't ask for a loan. It's my money.'

He dropped the envelope onto the bed.

'I can't take it. I'm sorry.'

'Please, Jaime, don't be so silly! It's my money, and I'm your partner. That means it's for both of us. That's what it's there for! Please, just take it! Pay off the bank and keep your house.'

The look of joy on Jaime's face at that moment was worth all the money in the world. In his happiness he hugged me so hard I felt I was being smothered.

'Darling, you can't imagine what this means to me. You've given me my life back. Thanks! Thanks a million! I don't know how to thank you, I really don't.'

'Well, you could show me this fabulous house you have in Madrid some time soon.'

As I said that, his eyes suddenly went blank for a moment, but then he focused lovingly on me once more.

'Of course I will!'

And that night, Jaime made love to me affectionately. The only problem was he could not wait, and it was all over before I could reach orgasm.

A Suite For Two

7th September 1998

How could I have guessed that Jaime had been looking through my personal papers and knew exactly how much money I had? We have never talked about money: for him it's taboo, and I have no problem with that. I have nothing to hide, but at the same time, I have not talked to him about my economic situation. The fact is that when the famous episode of the legal seizure of his goods was about to take place, the money Jaime needed was exactly the amount I had in my account. Jaime knew how much I had saved down to the last cent.

After the money crisis, things calmed down, and Jaime went on travelling for his work and for family reasons. I had no savings any more, but between my salary and what he earned, we lived well. Jaime continued to pay our outgoings, and every month he scrupulously gave me the money for the rent. We were living a second honeymoon, and the problem we had faced had only served to bring us closer together, and make our love all the stronger. That was what I thought, at least.

Today I set off for a famous fashion show in Italy, which my firm and I needed to attend. I knew Jaime was very much against the trip, especially following the argument we had over my boss's supposed intentions towards me. But Jaime did not stop me going. Until now I haven't given him any reason to feel jealous. I see the world through his eyes, and I live completely and exclusively for him. I've left my sordid sexual existence behind, and I no longer have any contact with my men friends.

When we arrived in Milan, a business associate of Harry, my boss, came and took us to our hotel. As we were driving into town, he told us there was a small problem about the rooms. All the hotels in the city were full, and the only thing he had managed to find for us was a large suite that we would have to share. I did not mind sharing a suite, as long as there were two beds in two different rooms. And that seemed to be the case, because when we got to the hotel we found that we could occupy the suite without being in each other's way at all, apart from sharing the bathroom. It was simply a matter of getting organized.

I told myself I was not even going to mention these arrangements to Jaime, because I knew he wouldn't understand. I did call him, though, to say I had arrived safely.

'Which hotel are you in?' he asked all of a sudden.

'The Westin Palace. Why?'

'Just to know. Give me the phone number and the number of your room. I'll call you, because it's very

153

expensive. I can see your boss is treating you like a princess: it's a lovely hotel!' he said.

I told Harry my boyfriend was about to call back, and warned him not to pick up the phone. I did not want to have to explain why it was Harry who had answered. Fortunately for me, Harry is a wonderful boss who understands these domestic matters perfectly.

A quarter of an hour later, Jaime was on the line.

'Who had the idea first?' he asked out of the blue.

'What idea?' I had no clue as to what he was talking about, but I feared the worst.

'Let me put it another way. Who fucked who?' he said, a sarcastic edge to his voice.

I couldn't say a word.

'Do you think I'm stupid? I spoke to the receptionist and asked him to put me through to your boss. By some extraordinary coincidence, he has the same room number as you. I called back, and they confirmed you are sharing a room.'

My heart started pounding. How could I convince him that things were not what they seemed?

'Jaime, I can explain. The thing is . . .'

'I don't want to hear your excuses. I want his version. Put him on!'

'No, Jaime! The two of us should talk about this. He's nothing to do with it . . .'

'Put him on!'

He was shouting so loudly that Harry, who was next to me, understood what was going on and asked me to pass him the phone.

When I heard Jaime shouting at him as well, I was so ashamed I did not know where to put myself. Harry looked at me, then concentrated on what Jaime was saying, only occasionally responding with a 'yes'. There are not many bosses as understanding and charming as he is ... I could tell that not only did he understand exactly what the situation was, but that he felt even worse about it than I did. As Jaime went on shouting over the phone, he was calmly smoking a cigar; and when the diatribe was over, he handed me the phone. Jaime wanted to give me precise instructions.

'Your beloved boss is going to find you another hotel. Once you've moved, you are to phone me with the new number and your hotel room. If he is a gentleman, he will find you something, however full the hotels are in Milan. I'll be waiting for you to call.'

He hung up. My tears started to fall onto the purple carpet of the suite. I tried to stammer out an excuse for what I had put Harry through. He went on chewing on his cigar, then stubbed it out and said to me, 'Don't worry. We'll sort this out right now.'

He made a few calls, and an hour later his associate took me to another hotel, about five hundred metres from the Westin. I did not call Jaime straight away, and by the time I did, he was furious. I told him the hotel phone number and my room number, and a few minutes later he called me back.

'What did you tell Harry?' I asked him, just as furious as he was.

'Just sufficient to make him behave properly. But I'll have to talk to him face to face when you two get back, so that he never tries anything with you again.'

This made me even more indignant. I didn't know what to say, but I felt extremely sad. The worst thing was

155

that I felt guilty about what had happened. We spent most of the night on the phone: he talked and talked about his philosophy of life, love, and above all about how much I still had to learn. I listened without saying a word. After we hung up, I found it impossible to get to sleep. I felt so humiliated and so ashamed towards Harry that I burst into tears once more. I was crying because I did not have the guts to tell Jaime how wrong he had been.

11th September 1998

I came back to Barcelona on my own: Harry took another flight for England. Jaime came to the airport to fetch me. He was carrying a big bunch of flowers, and he embraced me as though I had just been set free from a kidnapping. He told me how much he loved me, and explained that his behaviour was for my own good. For a long while I felt I could no longer look Harry in the face, because I was so ashamed of what I had put him through.

My Father Has Died . . .

9th December 1998

I think that on a few occasions, Jaime is beginning to realize how he has been behaving towards me. He suggested we spend a weekend in Menorca, perhaps to help me forgive him for what has happened. A reward for my patience, you deserve a rest, was how he put it. He said he would take care of everything, the air tickets and all the rest. He had been away all week in the north of Spain, and we were to leave tonight, Friday, for Mahon. The idea was that as soon as he got back, he would come to our apartment to pick me up.

I was excited, because this was the first weekend I was going to spend with him outside the city, so I sat in the living room waiting for him with my packed bag. Jaime phoned last night to tell me he would be reaching Barcelona at around five in the afternoon, and saying to make sure I was ready, because our plane left at half past seven. He wouldn't tell me what hotel we would be staying in: he wanted it to be a surprise.

By six o'clock there was still no sign of him. I called his mobile, but as usual it was switched off. I left a rather anxious message, saying I hoped he was just stuck in a typical Friday evening traffic jam. At half past six I rang his office, but his secretary had no news of him either. By now it was already too late to catch the plane, but I was more worried that he might have had an accident. I was imagining the worst. Jaime had been travelling with his partner Joaquin, so I called his mobile, but that was switched off too. I nearly had a heart attack, spending the evening phoning every hospital in Barcelona and surroundings to know if anyone called Rijas had been brought in. And every time a nurse said 'No', I heaved a huge sigh of relief. But I was increasingly mystified about what could have happened to him.

I spent the night sleeping on the couch. I turned up the volume on the telephone, so that when it rang in the early morning I woke up at once. It was Jaime.

'My father died of a heart attack yesterday evening,' he told me in a rough, grief-stricken voice.

The news felt like a blow to my stomach.

'My God! Where are you?'

'In the funeral parlour with my mother. I'm going to stay with her for a while. I'm sorry to have abandoned you, but . . .'

'Don't worry about that. Is there anything I can do for you? Do you want me to go there? Which funeral parlour are you in?'

'No, that's not a good idea. This is a real drama, I don't know how I'm going to cope with it. Give me some time to be with my mother, and then on my own. I'm feeling really bad.'

I told him again how sorry I was, and said I would wait for him at the apartment, for as long as it took. If he wants and needs to be alone, I can respect that.

15th December 1998

I go to work each day like a robot. I can't manage to concentrate on anything, and my boss Harry keeps asking what's wrong. I vaguely told him about a relative dying, without going into any details, and seeing how upset I was, he offered me some extra days off in addition to my Christmas leave.

I have no idea how long Jaime intends to stay away. Only one thing is clear: I miss him dreadfully, and I'm sincerely sorry for all that he is going through. I'm going to wait for him; I'm sure he'll show some sign of life before Christmas. We are supposed to be spending it together, because his children are going to be with their mother. But I have still had no news from him.

Week of the 24th December 1998 to 31st December 1998

This has been the worst Christmas of my entire life. I spent it at home, dragging the telephone with me wherever I went, waiting in vain for Jaime to surprise me and turn up at the last minute. But it didn't happen. I had a lot of time to think, and I have to say that at some point it seemed even to me that all this drama is a bit too strange to be true. But, almost immediately, I felt ashamed that I could doubt such a tragic event as the death of a loved one.

On New Year's Eve, Sonia tried to get me out of the house by inviting me to a party a former boyfriend of hers was organizing. I turned her down. She called again to find out how I was, but when she heard my tone of voice, she realized it was no use insisting.

Then Jaime reappeared, three weeks after the death. He has lost at least five kilos, and his face looks distinctly cadaverous. Yet his graceful slim fingers are so swollen he has difficulty closing his fist. And when he walks, his limp is more pronounced than ever. He has hardly spoken to me so far, and I don't dare talk to him. I can understand he is in mourning, and I have to respect that. Yet I would love to hug and kiss him and try to comfort him. Instead of that, consciously or not, he is becoming just another piece of furniture. He is crazier than ever. I suppose it must be grief making him that way. All this is bringing things to a head, and I'm beginning seriously to suspect that the man I fell in love with has nothing to do with the real man in front of me now.

Jaime has started to spend nights away. At first I put this down to his grief at losing his father, so I could not bring myself to say anything. But when he does come back at night he is usually completely drunk, and is looking to start a fight. As often as I can, I pretend to be asleep, and invariably he goes and locks himself in the bathroom, from where I can hear him scraping away with the scalpel. I pull the sheets up over my head, trembling and half dead with fear.

On those occasions when Jaime spends the night at home, his partner Joaquin usually turns up, and they both shut themselves in Jaime's study. Joaquin is always half drunk when he appears, and the evening always ends up in an argument because, from a conversation I once overheard, he asks Jaime for money to spend on prostitutes in clubs, or on the transvestites in Ciutadella.

Obsessions With Time

3rd January 1999

Tonight Jaime took a phone call which woke me up. He left the apartment in a hurry without a word to me. When he returned, the only explanation he gave was that his ex-wife had been very ill, and that his son had called him to come.

This is the second month that Jaime has forgotten to give me the rent. I have gone on paying it scrupulously. When I reminded him, Jaime asked me to wait a few days, but I know he's stopped taking responsibility for it. I get the sense he is falling into a deep depression, which he doesn't want to talk about.

4th January 1999

Today was one of the rare days when we had sex. Jaime had called up a prostitute and invited her back to the flat without asking my permission.

When I got in from work, he was sitting in the living

room chatting in a friendly way with a rough-looking woman. I understood what was going on straight away.

'It's a present for you, my love. I know I've been neglecting you lately . . .'

There was such a mixture of irony and tenderness in his voice, and I was so keen for him to desire me again, that I decided to go along with him, and agreed that the woman should stay for an hour.

For me the whole thing was a disaster. I felt completely inhibited, but Jaime was in his element. After the prostitute had left (I was the one who paid her) he was still aroused, and started fondling me.

'Let's see if I can't give you a baby!' he said, shutting himself in the bathroom to take a shower.

5th January 1999

I'm really worried about Jaime. His behaviour is getting more and more strange. He has always liked diaries, but until now I had not realized just how much. He is constantly buying all kinds of them, some leather-bound, others with cardboard covers, and then as soon as he has filled his latest purchase with his personal telephone numbers, all of them inscribed in his best handwriting, he buys another one and starts to copy it all out again. What a waste of time! And anyway, it serves no purpose. Even so, I try to justify it to myself by saying that it's better for someone to have a hobby than for them to have no interests at all. At least it's a way of keeping himself sane, I tell myself. Some people collect stamps; Jaime collects diaries.

I bought him one today, to console him for the fact that

I'm off on another trip. It's got light brown leather binding, with metal rings like a Filofax. I carefully put a photo of me inside the front cover, so that he can enjoy seeing me each time he opens it.

He seemed to have liked the diary, and walked all round the apartment with it in his hand.

6th January 1999

Today when I was taking the rubbish bag down to the bins I found the leather diary inside it. Jaime must have opened it when it was already taped up and hidden the diary so I would not see. I felt a stab of pain in my heart, and picked the diary out to look in it. All his personal telephone numbers were there, but he had made a mistake in one of them. He had crossed it out, and perhaps that was why he no longer liked the diary. My only consolation was that he seemed to have removed my photo. So at least he has kept that, probably in his wallet. I love him so much!

Watches are another passion. The other day he bought some smart wooden boxes that he piled up in his wardrobe, and in them he put all the watches he has been collecting over the years. Today I counted them. There are more than two hundred. I was so pleased to see how organized he is!

I am starting to feel both physically and psychologically ill. I feel sick the whole time. They have not noticed anything in the office, because I always have a bright smile. I think the sickness comes from the tension at home, because Jaime has still not completely recovered from his father's death.

7th January 1999

I feel terrible. Today I called a plumber because the toilet was blocked. For days now it has been filling up, and finally it seemed it might overflow. The plumber concluded that something was obstructing it, and after taking it apart for a hour, bits of the photograph I had put in Jaime's dairy came floating to the surface.

I wanted to find out more about Jaime. I went through his things, feeling guilty all the while. But I have to find some reason for why he is behaving so oddly.

I found letters returning unpaid cheques that Jaime had signed to pay for the apartment furniture. There were also telephone bills that he had paid, carefully placed in a file hidden among his other papers. They were so high he had obviously been unable to pay the most recent ones: there were more demanding letters. All the phone numbers were itemized, including one in Madrid that he seemed to have called every day at any time, but strangely enough not at the weekends, when he is supposed to be there.

I decided to try the number. I wanted to find out once and for all what was going on. I knew that what I was doing was wrong, but I felt I had to do it.

A soft young woman's voice answered. I did not hang up, but quickly asked if I could speak to Jaime Rijas.

'He's not here during the week, but he'll be here on Friday. Who is calling?'

'His wife,' I replied without thinking.

There was silence at the other end of the line. A few seconds later, I heard the voice again.

'Listen, I don't know who you are, but I'm Carolina, his girlfriend.'

The calm way she said this left me intrigued. I thought perhaps she imagined this was some kind of joke. Or perhaps she suspected as I did that Jaime was living a double life, and was not all that surprised at what she heard. I felt immediately attracted to her. She seemed like an intelligent person, free of the rancour so common in women who discover they are sharing a man.

'Carolina, I'm really sorry. My name is Val, and I'm Jaime's girlfriend here in Barcelona. We've been living together for several months now.'

This did sound like a joke, and I was afraid Carolina would not take me seriously.

Then all at once I felt very sick. Everything started spinning round, and I thought I was going to faint. I had to hang up and lie down for a while.

An hour later, I felt a lot better. I called Carolina again.

'I'm sorry. I suddenly felt faint and had to hang up. I apologize for inflicting myself on you like this. I'm not trying to claim Jaime is mine, but he's been so odd lately, I wanted to know what was wrong. Now I understand. I'm really sorry.'

'Don't worry,' she said in a friendly way. 'Jaime is someone who's always had lots of problems. But I really didn't think he would do anything like this.'

Again, I was amazed at how calm she was at the far end of the line. She went on, 'Jaime and I are only together at weekends, because his business is in Barcelona. I had no idea he was living with somebody else.'

I gave her my number, and we said goodbye. She

begged me not to say anything to Jaime, but we decided to get our own 'revenge' by arranging a meeting of all three of us without him knowing. Carolina told me Jaime intended to spend Valentine's Day in Madrid (how could he do that to me?) and if I agreed, I could go and see for myself what he has always kept hidden from me.

I have to admit that Carolina was always very correct with me. We did not fight, and she did not blame me for anything. In the end, we're in the same boat. The only person to blame for this situation is Jaime: we are nothing more than two innocent victims, madly in love with the same man. It was a struggle, but I managed to keep my discovery a secret until the date I had arranged to go and meet Carolina.

Meanwhile, I was feeling increasingly nauseous every morning, and I began to fear the worst.

The Contract

Jaime is torturing me more and more. Perhaps he can sense something. Tonight he had a business dinner with his partner and a possible client. He insisted I went too, and that I should make myself 'sexy'.

'For a business dinner?'

'Yes, he's a very special client and I need your help for once.'

'What kind of help?'

'I want you to be friendly, that's all. Is that too much to ask?'

I could see he was getting angry again, so I agreed to go to the dinner to avoid an argument. On our way there, Jaime explained about the client.

'I've been chasing him for ages, but he always slams the door shut in my face. But the fact that he's having dinner with us means we have the chance of signing a contract.'

Jaime and Joaquin had agreed to meet up beforehand

to settle what they should say, and how to direct the meal to convince the client he should sign the three-million-peseta contract with them.

The bar was a tiny, exclusive place, with an entrance like a ship's gangway. Inside, a narrow staircase led to a small room with a huge teak bar that took up over half the space. There were a lot of people there already, so we did not have much room. I did not like the atmosphere and I suppose my unease showed, because Jaime several times asked me to smile.

Joaquin was already installed at one corner of the bar, deep in discussion with two heavily made-up young ladies. When they saw Jaime, the two of them greeted him as though they had known him all their lives. They looked me up and down scornfully and decided to ignore me completely, as if I did not even exist. I stayed behind Jaime, partly due to the lack of room, and partly because the two women intimidated me. I played no part in the conversation, but I could see the conniving way that Joaquin was glancing at Jaime. They seemed to be saying something to each other that only they could grasp. I could not understand Jaime's attitude, especially after what he had told me about the way Joaquin had used him over the bank loan. That did not seem to have affected their friendship in the least.

I don't like Joaquin. I have never warmed to him, not even the first day I saw him. He is tall, with completely white hair. He always wears brightly coloured ties and big brown plastic glasses like Onassis. Gruesome! You can smell his pipe from a mile away, whether he has it lit or not. Joaquin is a member of a rich bourgeois Catalan family that is on the way down. He lives on the outskirts of Barcelona in a beautiful mansion his wife owns. He has been out on the town for months now, and tonight he was flirting openly with the two women at the bar. Seeing my long face, all at once he turned towards me and declared, 'You're too young to understand certain things. You've still got a lot to learn.'

It wasn't worth me protesting. But I started to feel a mounting anger towards Jaime, who did nothing to defend me or put Joaquin in his place.

After our drinks we set off for the restaurant, where their client was already waiting for us. Jaime drew me to one side and whispered, 'Joaquin is already drunk, so we can't let him talk too much over dinner. It's up to you and me to deal with the client, right?'

'Me?'

'Yes, I need your help. You're more intelligent than you think, you'll see.'

What on earth did he mean by that? The client was sitting smoking a cigarette at a table for four in a corner of the restaurant. We said hello, and Jaime presented me as an office associate. I did not say anything, because I imagined this must be part of a strategy of his for keeping his business affairs and his private life separate. Jaime pressed me to take a seat next to the client.

There was lots of lively debate over dinner, but I hardly dared open my mouth. The client, a small, slimy character, did not stop drinking or staring at my legs. I began to feel offended, because I could see Jaime had noticed what was going on, and had done nothing to protect me. He has always been jealous, but now it was a question of a three-million-peseta contract, he did not say a word.

After dessert, the client started stroking my legs under

the table, still talking animatedly to Jaime. I was petrified. I could see Joaquin was calmly lighting his pipe, oblivious to whatever was going on. I could not believe my eyes when I glanced at Jaime and he gave me little nods to show I should carry on. Instinctively, all my muscles stiffened, and when the client started to slide his hand up the inside of my thigh, I stood up and threw my napkin down onto the table. I could not control myself any longer, so I shouted at Jaime, 'Am I only worth three million pesetas to you?' The whole restaurant turned to look in my direction.

Jaime feigned surprise.

'What's wrong?'

'This ape has got his hands all over me; aren't you going to do anything about it?'

Jaime looked across at the client, who had dropped his hands by his sides.

'Just behave!' he said, leaving me completely deflated.

Joaquin sat puffing away at his pipe, a silly smile on his face.

'What did you say?' I roared.

'I said, behave!' Jaime ordered me. 'You're ruining everything!'

I did not know what hurt me more: their client's pawing or Jaime's attitude. I was so indignant I left the table, asked for my coat and ran out of the restaurant. So Jaime would have been happy to share me with a stranger. I felt like throwing up.

I cried all the way home. When Jaime came in at five in the morning as if nothing at all had happened, it was at last clear to me that he doesn't love me and in fact never has.

Before he slipped into bed beside me, while I was pretending to be still asleep, he whispered, 'You're very young still. You have a lot to learn.'

His presence next to me revolted me. I'm not going to be able to put up with this much longer.

The Worst Is Yet To Come

9th January 1999

The pharmacy was crowded, so I sat on a chair next to the counter. My period was a week late, and even before I took the test I knew I was pregnant, although I tried hard to convince myself I couldn't be. I can tell by the tiny heartbeats I feel down near my right ovary, and although Sonia protests and says it's impossible to feel anything like that for several months, I know for sure there is something growing inside me. I haven't said anything to Jaime. I'm worried what his reaction might be, even though it was obvious it might happen because we haven't taken any precautions for some time now. Also, one day he told me he would love to be a father again now that he feels mature, and that it would have to be now or never, otherwise he would feel like a grandfather rather than a father. Of course, I was right. The pregnancy test did not even take the time meant to be necessary to change colour. As soon as I dipped the indicator into my urine, it turned positive. I couldn't be more pregnant.

I told Jaime tonight. He sat staring at me as if he had seen a ghost. I was ready for any reaction: joy or rage. What I had not expected was for him to say, 'That's impossible!'

'Why is it impossible? Here's the proof.'

I showed him the test, which I had put away in its aluminium case.

'I'm telling you, it's impossible!' he repeated, without accepting what his eyes were seeing. His voice was so mocking I started to tremble. 'I don't doubt that you're pregnant. What I doubt is that it's mine.'

I only just stopped myself leaping at him. That was just the kind of reaction he must have been expecting. I sat very still and calm, though my heart was in my mouth.

'How can you say that, Jaime? Ever since I've known you, you're the only person I've slept with.'

'I doubt that,' he replied seriously. I could see he was getting angry.

'How can you say such a thing?'

'Quite simply, because I'm sterile.'

I have often had bad moments with Jaime. Sometimes I have hated him with all my being, or felt angry or powerless, but today I could feel the whole structure of our relationship come crashing down around me. This must all be some huge joke. I couldn't find any other explanation. I ran to the bathroom to be sick and while I was bent over with my head in the toilet bowl, furiously trying to clear my mind, I heard Jaime's voice behind me. He went on with his explanation, 'I've been sterile for years. I was lucky enough to be able to have two children, but I'll never have another one. So stop all this pretence, and admit you've slept with someone else!'

I did not know what to say. He had become a complete monster to me, and I did not want to talk to him.

'I wouldn't be surprised if you hadn't slept with your boss, and now you want me to take on the burden.'

Every word he said was like a punch to my chin. I was sick a second time.

'Or maybe you're making it with my partner. Ah, now I understand why Joaquin is always here these days! I shouldn't have trusted you!'

I wanted to object, but I was so hurt all I could do was scream.

'Now you're getting hysterical. Just look at you! And don't think I don't know what you get up to when I'm in Madrid at the weekends!'

I could have told him I had spoken to Carolina and knew about his double game, but I found it impossible to say a word. Because I didn't reply, he became even more angry and cruel.

'Condemned by your silence! You disgust me!'

The words echoed round the apartment as he stormed out.

My Unhappy Valentine

14th February 1999

I had an abortion. Silently, alone, although a baby is what I most long for in the world. The day I told Jaime I was pregnant and he stormed out, I found a psychiatric report among his papers, with questions he had answered. One of the replies said that what would make him happiest of all would be to spend the entire week with Carolina, but that she could not stand him any longer, and that he had fallen foul of his cocaine habit again. There were other replies that I prefer to forget because they were so cruel. Yet what he wrote about women caught my attention: he said he hated them all apart from his mother. The psychiatrist's conclusion was that Jaime was in a schizophrenic state: a bipolar disorder brought on by the destruction of his brain cells caused by the cocaine habit. He recommended a stay in a specialized clinic for treatment.

I could not bear to bring a baby into a world so full of madness, with a crazy drug addict for a father. I was afraid all this might affect the child, and I was horrified at the thought I might have to go on having links with this raving madman, who was capable of harming both the baby and me.

The day before yesterday, Jaime rang. He threatened that if I did not have the abortion, he would 'fuck up' my life. I believe him. He would do anything so long as he came out of it all right.

Today I took the shuttle plane to Madrid to meet Carolina. I told her about the baby on the phone, and she was very upset, as Jaime had done the same to her. A few years ago. He isn't sterile. He invented that nonsense in order to put off any woman who tried emotional black-mail on him in that way – not that I was doing that of course. All I want now is to get rid of this albatross around my neck, to get rid of my love for him, to start a new life. In order to do that, I need to exorcize him by talking to the person who knew him best, the woman with whom he shared his life.

Carolina suggested the two of us meet up in a bar. I was very nervous about seeing her for the first time. We recognized each other at once, instinctively: unhappi-ness in a face is unmistakable. For the first few minutes I felt very uncomfortable. Carolina is much older than I am, and is incredibly beautiful and gentle. In a way, I was flattered that Jaime should want to deceive her with me, but I soon dismissed such nonsense from my mind and focused again on the sad reality that he had been constantly manipulating me, and had never loved me.

Carolina and I needed a stiff drink in order to be able to tell each other all we know about Jaime. I began to describe how we had met, the problem that arose when his house was about to be seized, his father's death, his nocturnal drinking and his sudden disappearing acts.

Carolina was listening very carefully to all this, her black eyes opening wide every time she could identify with something I was saying.

'The only time I ever heard anything about you was when Jaime told me he had taken on a French girl at the office,' she said when she realized I had finished.

'I've never worked in his office. I didn't want to.'

'His father's funeral never happened. He's not dead, but lives in a shack with no electricity. Jaime is from a very poor family, and hasn't spoken to his father in years. When I met Jaime, he tried that funeral trick on me too, until I discovered the truth. I'm sure he needed an excuse to go off for a few days with some girl or other, so he made up the whole dreadful lie. Jaime is a compulsive liar. Before Christmas, he and I were travelling in the Canary Islands. That's why he invented the story about his father dying. I'm so sorry!'

Her words reverberated round the inside of my head.

'And as for the chalet, it doesn't belong to him. My husband bought it when we married. On his death, I inherited it. Jaime came to live with me there. But it belongs to me, and there was never any risk of a legal seizure. He was lying to you about that too.'

I could not believe anyone would stoop so low.

'What about his children? He told me he spent every weekend here with his two children.'

'His children don't even want to see him. For months now they have only spoken to him when it's absolutely necessary.'

'So what were the five million pesetas I gave him for?'

Carolina's expression told me she did not have the faintest idea.

'I gave him five million to prevent his house being seized!' I shouted.

'It seems to me he just wanted to get money out of you.'

So as well as being a liar, Jaime is a cheat.

'Jaime has always had money problems. He spends it like water. He lives the life of a lord. For years it was me who kept him, until I had enough of it. It's been two years since I last helped him out. Since then he's been getting lots of demands, from his associates, from all kinds of people. I don't want to know. I imagine he was looking for someone else to wheedle money from. The same thing happened with his wife. In the end she grew tired of it, and threw him out. Now she wants to live in peace and quiet and have nothing to do with the scoundrel. I'm sorry to be so blunt, but it's all I can say.'

'His ex-wife is very ill, isn't she?'

'Not at all. Carmen is in perfect health. So he told you too she had cancer, did he? Not a bit of it. She's fine; the only thing she wants is to wipe out all the years she spent with that gentleman. I'm trying to do the same, but I'm still very much in love with him and can't.'

I wanted to die on the spot. I'm a woman who has been betrayed, deceived, ruined, and destroyed both physically and mentally. And I was with a woman who had suffered the same, but seemed to have forgiven her lover almost all her humiliation. Carolina told me she had agreed to meet Jaime in the bar opposite, and that she had to go because he might turn up at any moment. Just then, my mobile rang. It was Jaime.

'Even though I'm not with you, I was ringing to wish you a happy Valentine's Day,' he said.

How could anyone be so cynical? I had to force myself not to reveal where I was.

'Where are you?' I asked in a strangled voice.

'I'm spending the weekend with my mother, in Barcelona.'

I didn't say where I was. He had no idea I might be in Madrid with Carolina. When we had said goodbye, Carolina commented, 'You see what a liar he is? He's on his way to the bar.'

This time it was her mobile that rang. Surprised, she glanced at me; then we both realized it must be Jaime.

'Fine,' she said. 'I'll see you in ten minutes.'

She switched off. Jaime had just told her he was coming out of the metro, on his way to meeting her. We exchanged looks again, unable to believe anyone could be so two-faced.

I don't know how I found the strength to turn up at the bar twenty minutes later. I was split between the wish either to run away, or to stay and explain to him I had discovered what kind of a person he really was. I am still in love with him, but I wanted to teach him a lesson for all that he has done not only to me, but to Carolina as well.

I walked into the bar like a zombie. Jaime was so astonished it took him several minutes to react. I felt terrible, with the strange sensation that I was an unwelcome intruder into the privacy of a couple who had nothing to do with me. Carolina pushed a chair towards me, and asked Jaime if he knew who I was. He did not know what to say. He turned green when he realized that for the first time in his life he had been caught out, that someone had stripped off his mask. He tried to get up several times, as if to escape from our little triangle, but each time I pulled him back down. The other people in the bar didn't know whether to be amused or shocked at the soap opera they were witnessing, but none of them intervened. Jaime finally managed to run off, and Carolina suggested I went with her to her house, situated in a famous residential development about twenty kilometres outside Madrid. She wanted to show me where they lived. She said I could even spend the night there, as Jaime was unlikely to put in another appearance.

Despite still feeling like an intruder, I accepted, partly because I thought she probably didn't want to be on her own. It was as though there was a kind of involuntary complicity between us. I owed it to her, I felt, as a way of thanking her for her attitude towards me.

When we got to the chalet, we proceeded to get drunk on gin. Then Carolina wanted to show me the bedroom.

Perhaps I accepted her offer to stay over because I wanted to see how Jaime lived, in order to try to understand him a bit better. But what exactly was there to understand? I had no idea. The house was full of photographs of Carolina and him.

'Memories of happy moments we spent together,' she said nostalgically. 'Of course, it's been years now since I felt good with him, but I can't get rid of him. I can tell him on the phone I have had enough, but as soon as he reappears I fall into the trap again. This isn't a life. At least, it's not the life I wanted for me or for my children.'

At some point, while we were still drinking to help us

bear the pain of so much love for such a perverse creature, Jaime called Carolina's mobile again. He wanted to beg her forgiveness. He did not know of course that we were both in his house. All she said was that she wanted him to move out once and for all, but Jaime kept begging her not to throw him out, not to abandon him, saying he had never loved me. That I was nothing more than a mistake. Ten minutes later, he phoned me. He tried exactly the same story with me: he said he'd never loved Carolina, she was a poor widow left alone in this world with her children, he felt sorry for her, but he wanted to get back together with me. He asked me to forgive him for all the hurt he had caused me. I couldn't even listen to half his excuses, and cut off the call. Carolina and I were drunk by now, but that did not make us any less indignant. How low could anyone go?

'I've got an idea,' Carolina said, a malicious gleam in her eyes, just as I was about to fall into a drunken sleep. 'The worst thing anyone can do to Jaime is to touch his things. Come and look . . .'

She led me to their room, where Jaime had left all his things. In his wardrobe I was surprised to find the same wooden boxes he had in our Barcelona flat for storing all his watches. So he had recreated his Madrid house in our apartment. We were so angry we took out his clothes and Carolina started cutting them up with a pair of scissors. I did the same with his silk ties, which he had carefully hung on several hangers. We put all the pieces into plastic bags, then Carolina got out a suitcase to put them all in. She wrote Jaime's name on a label. Despite ourselves, we had just become accomplices in an act of vandalism.

Carolina called a hotel and reserved a room in the name of Rijas. She told the receptionist that a suitcase would arrive for him, and that it should be given to him as soon as he arrived. We got out the car and drove straight to the hotel to drop off the case. Then she sent him a text message telling him the address of the hotel where she had left all his things. Jaime did not have the nerve to reply. I'll never forget that moment in all my life. Because of the tension we had felt for more than twenty-four hours, Carolina and I started to laugh hysterically at the thought of Jaime's face when he saw what we had done to his clothes.

An Unhappy Ending

15th February 1999

I said goodbye to Carolina, asking her to forgive me for having burst into her life in this way. All I was trying to do was to understand Jaime in order to break free of the love spell he had cast on me. I had no wish to harm her in any way; she was no more than a poor slave to a selfish monster who felt only anger towards all women.

I suppose that, as time goes by, Carolina will end up hating me.

3rd March 1999

I have to get out of the apartment. I can't go on paying the rent and the heavy expenses, and besides, I can't live here any more. Every room reminds me of Jaime and his crazy behaviour. I wrote to the agency, telling them we were going to hand back the apartment because we had separated. According to the contract, I have to pay them compensation because we have not been here a year. I'm responsible because I was the one who signed. I'm finding all this kind of thing extremely difficult. At night I can hardly sleep, and I'm in a nervous state the whole time. I'm still in touch with Carolina. She calls me frequently to tell me Jaime follows her to work every day, begging her to forgive him and take him back. Up to now, she has refused. But I know she will end up falling into his arms again. It's hard to resist Jaime. She'll go back to him because she's afraid of ending up alone, and he needs her because he's completely lost, and Carolina is the only person who really knows him.

April 1999

I have moved fairly rapidly to a much smaller flat on the other side of town from the Olympic Village. I called the removal firm to come one morning, but the previous evening Jaime got in while I was out and took all the valuables from the apartment. In other words, he's left me with next to nothing. I was almost grateful, because in my new place there is hardly any room. I've gone from an apartment of a hundred and twenty square metres to a flat of about fifty square metres, hidden away in the city. I came across it by chance on one of my walks around Barcelona.

To get revenge, Jaime also destroyed the marble worktop in the kitchen. I don't know how he did it, but it's caused me a huge headache with the owner, who obviously is asking me to pay for it to be repaired. My situation could not be worse. I have no savings, I have debts everywhere because of Jaime's wrecking of the apartment, and on top of all that, I've left my job with

Harry. I resigned because I knew I couldn't do it properly feeling as bad as I do. It would not have been professional of me to carry on. Above and beyond all this, I feel completely destroyed: all I have left in the world are the bitter memories of being in love with someone who never loved me, who simply laughed at me, took advantage of me, and who cheated me in every sense.

Strangely, I don't feel at all jealous of Carolina. On the contrary, I think we felt a certain solidarity from the moment we met. She never called into question what I told her about my relationship with Jaime, and I'll always be grateful to her for the way she opened her house to me. In the end, I'm nothing more than a stranger to her who burst into her world and brought part of it crashing down.

Jaime has tried to speak to me several times. He knows where I've moved to, because he followed me as well. One night, he rang the doorbell. I felt such a pang of the love that I still feel for him that I let him in. He was drunk. He begged me to forgive him, and told me he had ended everything with Carolina. I knew this was a lie, because Carolina and I are still in touch. He also told me his business was on the rocks, and that he needed money. He was trying to pull the wool over my eyes once more, but finally I managed to throw him out into the street.

I still do not really understand why Jaime had to do this to me. He has lots of women at his feet, and many of them are far richer than me.

I discovered that the jar of powder he said was from a pharmacy, for treating his ankle, was in fact pure cocaine. Even over this, I tried to find reasons to excuse him. Because I still love him. From now on I have to fight against two enemies: firstly, against him and the memory of him; and secondly, against myself, and falling back under his spell.

August 1999

Several months have gone by while I have felt lethargic, incapable of doing anything. I can hardly remember what has happened. I shut myself up in my flat, without even bothering to move my furniture from where it was stacked against the walls. I haven't been eating; I simply let myself float along. I want to annihilate myself. I'm letting myself die; one night I prayed with all my remaining strength that the end would not be long in coming.

The Brothel

A place where the vulnerability and frailty of human beings are always on show

I was thirty when I decided to enter the brothel. It followed my break-up with Jaime. I could not forgive him for leaving me with an empty bank account and life-long debts, or the fact that he had left me for a bimbo who could never grow up. I was devastated, because all my beliefs about true love had suddenly evaporated.

I had been considering the possibility day and night for at least six months. I had thought of it before over the years, but never got round to doing anything about it. I suppose I needed something extra to give me the courage to take the first step. Women of all social classes (I know this from talking to friends) have considered prostitution at some point in their lives. We rarely act on the idea, however, because it seems as though it is no more than part of our erotic fantasies. I certainly had experienced fantasies along those lines, but I was always scared when I saw the women involved. I thought they lived in a grey, violent world, victims of a pimp who kept watch on them twenty-four hours a day.

Immediately after my separation, I had wanted to die. But I found it so hard to commit suicide in peace! For whatever reason, there was always something or someone who, usually without even realizing it, got in the way of that most intimate act, our right to die when we want.

Once when I tried to throw myself out of a window, Bigudi, who was back with me, started to meow to be fed. She was so insistent with her cries, and the way she scratched at my trouser leg, that I had to give up.

On another occasion, when I tried to take two boxes of sleeping pills, the water to my flat had been cut off. I searched desperately for some mineral water or a sip of alcohol, but there wasn't so much as a drop in the whole place. I decided to put it off to the next day, but the old saying 'don't put off until tomorrow what you can do today' proved true yet again.

Gradually my desire to die wore off. In its place I felt only apathy, sadness, and a deep, deep depression.

Six months went by. I literally shut myself in my flat, with the shutters closed, going from my bed to the bathroom, the bathroom to my bed. I was never hungry, only thirsty, because I got into the habit of getting drunk with the excuse that there was nothing wrong with drinking: it helped you find another reality and did no one else any harm.

I had always been a strong, resolute woman, but after I left Jaime I resigned from my job in Harry's company. And because I had no money, I had to move to a part of Barcelona I had never frequented before. I left my beautiful loft in the Olympic Village, and before I moved in to my new fifty-metre-square flat, I spent a week in a cheap boarding house in the Paralelo district, living out of my suitcase. I had Bigudi under one arm, a case full of memories under the other, and a medical certificate from an abortion clinic in my pocket. Women only have crises through love or the loss of a child. The rest, they can cope with. And now because of love I found myself lost and alone in the world, living next to some very shady characters and with cheap prostitutes in the street out-side, in an area full of bars and homeless people.

I watched all this teeming life from my window. I was particularly fascinated by the prostitutes, and felt glad each morning when I recognized one of their faces. I got to know them – without ever speaking to them (I would have died of shame) – and came to feel they were keep-ing me company. At some level or other, I could understand them. I had always believed that to make ends meet it was better to sell your body than to work every weekend like a slave in a bar, twelve hours a day for a pittance. When I was doing Business Studies at university, a lot of my fellow students nearly killed themselves working as waiters in order to pay for their studies and live decently. I was lucky: I had a scholar-ship, and received economic support from my parents each month.

Now, as the days went by, I grew tired of living like a sewer rat in the boarding house. I started very occasion-ally to go out into the street. As I went downstairs, I could see the real world opening before me. I never took the lift, because the pink plush paper lining it made me feel very claustrophobic. I was scared of getting stuck inside, unable to breathe, and being trapped by these chewing-gum walls, flailing with my arms to try to free myself from the sticky mess entangling me.

In the end, I succeeded in the goal I had set myself after my break-up with Jaime. I killed somebody. I killed the well-behaved, studious, ambitious person I had inside me. I killed her because I instinctively knew that if I did, I would set free another much more human and sensitive being, one with far more curiosity about life.

There's Always A First Time

1 September 1999

The first contact I had with the brothel was the result of a final instinct for survival, or perhaps for self-destruction, depending on how you look at it. I'm not sure, but I think we human beings always try to preserve ourselves. So I prefer to believe it was the first option that took me there.

What I found was very different from the glamorous picture I had in my imagination. The girls turned out to be little Cinderellas, except that they never lost glass slippers, but a part of themselves. There was a huge contrast between how innocent some of them were and the way they made love to their clients. This physical contrast stupefied me.

I was one of the oldest, and knew what I was doing. A lot of them worked in the brothel to earn as much money as possible – not because they needed to, but because they hated the idea of being poor and thought you could buy happiness with banknotes. Above all, I was looking for affection and to try to recover my self-esteem, but deep down we all had the same wish: to find love.

Two thirty in the afternoon.

At last I had got out of the boarding house. I was walking along the street, counting the slabs of pavement, incapable of thinking straight about anything.

This morning I bought a newspaper and cut out an advert for a luxury establishment offering the most beautiful and elegant girls in the city. I didn't think twice about it, but called at once to see if they needed any new people, because I was interested in working with them. They told me the address and asked me to come in the afternoon.

I wanted to get there was quickly as possible, to see this world I had so often imagined. I visualized myself in a luxury apartment filled with silk drapes, dressed in a transparent nightie, with themed bedrooms and jacuzzis in every bathroom.

Ten to three.

When Susana opened the door, I excused myself, saying I must have come to the wrong address. She said no, I had come to the right place, and showed me in.

Susana was a small, fat, ugly redhead. She was holding a cigarette in nicotine-stained fingers. Worse still, all her teeth looked like jagged black rocks about to fall out.

'Surely that scares the clients off?' I thought.

'Do you smoke?' she asked straight out, without so much as a 'hello'.

'Yes, thanks,' I said, taking a cigarette nervously from her. My hands were trembling, and this was the first and only time she offered me a cigarette, because I soon became the person who supplied her need for tar and nicotine.

In spite of the fact that I knew exactly where I was, I still did not know for sure whether I was there out of a sense of vengeance, because I was so disgusted with men and what they have dangling between their legs, or because I needed affection and a boost to my self-esteem, not to mention my money worries. I suppose it was a mixture of all those reasons, and in addition I've always thought of myself as a liberal-minded woman, so the idea of becoming a prostitute did not cause me any great trauma or frighten me.

'If you just wait a minute,' Susana said, looking me up and down, 'the boss will be here. Then she can meet you personally. I'm Susana, the day manager.'

I suddenly noticed something on the floor by the door to the apartment. It was a lemon, with matches and a lit cigarette sticking in it.

'It attracts clients,' Susana explained, laughing. 'It's a bit of witchcraft. Cindy taught it me.'

'Cindy?'

'A Portuguese girl who works here. I'll introduce you to her. She's got all kinds of tricks, and they all work.' Susana seemed very convinced of this.

When she showed me into a small room where the only furniture was a bed and an oval mirror surrounded by lights, I suddenly began to feel afraid, as if something dreadful might happen to me. I had a knot in my stomach, and a strange feeling that I could not breathe. My mouth was dry as dust.

'You wouldn't have a glass of water, would you?' I asked Susana.

'Yes, sweetheart, you just sit on the bed and wait for the boss, and I'll bring you the water, OK?'

She seemed a good sort. She looked awful, but there must have been some reason why she was in here.

The room was ghastly: the complete opposite of what I had imagined. The walls were covered in a peeling yellow wallpaper, while from the ceiling hung a pink curtain presumably intended to give an air of intimacy and old-fashioned luxury, but failing to do either. Several of the lights around the mirror had gone out, but I could not help staring at myself in it. I suddenly felt myself falling into a kind of mild schizophrenia that was taking me to a different world, one where the language of words had no meaning, where everything was measured by the body and its sensations. The woman reflected in the sad mirror was someone I did not know. I saw the face of a woman who has landed somewhere she was not meant to, but is determined to make it on her own in spite of everything. The stubborn face of a woman who wanted to justify this choice to herself at all costs.

'Here's your water,' Susana said, coming silently into the room. In her other hand, the filter-tip was almost burning her fingers.

I was still staring at myself in the mirror, but Susana's entrance brought me back to reality with a bump.

'Hi there,' I heard a voice with a gentle English accent say from behind Susana.

'Hello,' I replied, anxious to discover the face that fitted such a kind voice.

A small dark pregnant woman held out her hand to me. I was astonished. How come such a pleasant woman, about to have a baby, was the madam of a brothel like this? I had never imagined anything of the sort. It was the last thing I had been expecting, and I even found myself disappointed not to be faced with a man looking like a truck driver, and covered in tattoos. The newcomer's obvious gentleness and vulnerable condition did not seem to fit at all with such a decadent atmosphere.

'I'm Cristina. I'm the owner.'

'Hello, I'm Val.'

'Susana tells me you want to work with us.'

'Yes, I'd like to.'

'Where have you worked before?'

'You mean, in this kind of work?'

'Of course. What other brothels have you worked in?' Cristina insisted.

I did not know whether to lie or tell the truth.

'I've never done this kind of work before. This is my first time.'

Cristina and Susana both stared at me, and I could see from their eyes that they didn't believe a word of what I had said.

'Are you sure you'll be able to do it?' Cristina asked. 'Our girls here are very professional.'

'I can try.'

I said this so firmly that Cristina seemed convinced.

'All right,' she said. 'Susana, have we got a dress she can wear for now?'

'Yes, but I think it's Estefania's. If she hears we've borrowed it, she'll be mad at me.'

'Go and fetch it. I'll take the responsibility. This girl here can't receive any clients dressed the way she is.'

'You mean I'm going to start right now?' I said, beginning to panic.

'Didn't you say you wanted to work?' Cristina replied, smiling broadly.

'Of course, it's just that I never imagined it would be so quickly.'

'That's the best way, believe me. Otherwise, how long are you going to wait? There's a very good client waiting in the salon. He comes every week. If he likes a girl, he spends two hours with her. So it's up to you. He pays a hundred thousand pesetas, and you'll get fifty thousand.'

'OK!'

Susana came back in with a long red transparent dress, deeply cut at the front, and the lingerie to match.

'Try these on, sweetheart. But hurry up, the client is waiting,' Cristina urged me. 'I've told him we have a new girl, a model who's only in Barcelona for a few days. He's dying to meet you.'

'Fine,' I replied, stepping out of my jeans without a further thought. 'What do I have to do with him?'

'That's up to you,' replied Susana. 'He's a bit of a nuisance because he's drugged to the eyeballs. In general though he doesn't want the whole works, because he's impotent. A good masturbation should keep him happy.'

'I'm to masturbate him for two hours?'

'No, not for two hours,' Cristina said, laughing. 'Give him some foreplay, a massage, whatever. It's up to you to arouse him. Come on, get dressed and don't worry, everything will be all right. And put some make-up on, you look very pale. Our clients like their women well-turned out. The opposite of what they have at home. Why would they want to pay a woman who looks exactly like their wife?'

'I see,' I said, pulling on the dress.

With the dress on, the image I could see in the mirror did not look all that different from someone who had done herself up to go out on a first date with a man. I was reassured, but my heart was still beating furiously, as though it were terrified.

'See how gorgeous she looks in that dress!' Susana exclaimed, drawing her boss's attention to me.

'She's fantastic!' Cristina agreed. 'You've got a lovely body, you should take advantage of it. A bit lacking around the breasts perhaps, but you can sort that out when you've got your first million!'

I didn't appreciate her remark about my breasts in the slightest, but I wasn't going to let her see that. It was no time to get into an argument.

'If you play your cards right, you can earn a lot of money. You'll see, you'll get on fine with us. Get along with you now, we'll talk afterwards.'

Susana took my hand like a little girl, gave my make-up the once-over, then took me to a salon I hadn't seen before. The décor was similar to the room I had been in at first. There was a big chintz sofa and next to it a glass coffee table with copper legs shaped like vines. A few copies of *Playboy* lay open on it, as if someone had been flicking through them. There was a single matching arm-chair in the far corner. Two doors led into the salon: one was painted white, the other was a wooden sliding door. I guessed this led to another bedroom.

'There's a suite in there,' explained Susana, as proud

as if she owned the whole place. 'That's where the client is. You'll see it later on. And this is the bathroom,' she opened the white door to show me. 'Now, take a seat and I'll bring the client in.'

She knocked gently at the wooden door, then opened it a little way, so that I could not make out what was inside. Then she vanished, as though swallowed up by this mysterious room. I heard whispers and could hear the impatient protests of a man, annoyed because he had been made to wait so long. My heart was racing.

A few minutes later, and Susana came out again. Her cheeks were flushed.

'I don't like going in there,' she said, giggling behind her hand. 'The client is naked. Go in when you like, sweetheart, he's paid me.'

She showed me the banknotes in her hand.

'I'll give you your cut afterwards.'

As she left the room she shot me a knowing look, and I was surprised when she added, 'Enjoy yourself, sweetheart.'

I stood at the door for a moment, holding my breath. I was not worried about going to bed with a stranger. What really scared me was the thought that he might not like me; my self-esteem was absolutely at zero. I thought it would be a tremendous failure if I was rejected the first time. I made up my mind, and knocked firmly at the door. A voice shouted, 'Get in here! Otherwise time is passing and we won't have done anything.'

When I stepped inside, I found him lying on his back on the bedcover, totally naked. The room was too dark for me to make out his prick properly. He looked quite young, thirty-five years old at the most. What Susana so proudly called the suite was nothing more than a bedroom with red velvet wallpaper, thick curtains that kept out all natural light, and a king-size bed. On either side of the bed was a table like the one in the salon, decorated with bronze naked female figures eating grapes. The whole of the wall opposite the bed was a mirror, giving the distinct impression that this was a Parisian *maison close*. I thought this kind of place would have changed over the years, and done away with such typical bad taste.

'Let me get a good look at you,' the client said, getting up from the bed. 'You're new, aren't you?'

'Yes. I've just arrived.'

'That's what they all say, and that they've never done this before. Then you run into them in all the agencies in Barcelona. But maybe you're telling the truth. I haven't seen you before. If you'd been working anywhere else, I'd have noticed you. Shall we have a bath together?'

He went over to the jacuzzi in the corner of the room and turned on the taps.

'What's your name?' he asked, feeling to test the water temperature.

'Val,' I replied, still not moving towards him.

'That's nice! I haven't heard it before. You're a foreigner, aren't you?' Then he added, almost inaudibly, 'Like all the rest, anyway.'

'Yes, I'm French.'

'French and not exactly a talker. That's good. Girls usually talk too much and it's all nonsense. I'm Alberto. Come over here so I can see you better. You seem very shy.'

'No, I'm not shy. It's just that this is such an odd place.'

'I get it,' Alberto said indulgently, then stepped into the jacuzzi. 'Take your clothes off and get in with me.'

I must admit that the idea of taking a bath with a strange man in such an overused installation revolted me a little, but what choice did I have? If I've decided to do this, I have to go the whole way.

I undressed quickly, rocking my body to and fro in the borrowed lingerie in order to get up my courage faced with this stranger whom I had nothing against, but who, for the moment at least, could not arouse any passion in me.

'Wow! You French girls are something else. Come and move like that in the water, will you?'

I got in next to him. The water was very hot, and I hesitated before sitting down. Alberto grabbed me by the waist and pulled me to him.

'Come here. I want to feel you.'

He began to fondle my breasts, soaping them with the bath gel he had squirted into the jacuzzi. Then, under the water, his fingers started groping between my legs. In spite of my liberal views, I didn't really know how these things were supposed to happen. I was a bit taken aback by the situation: whereas before it was me who chose the men I wanted, now my opinion did not come into it. They were the ones who decided what was going to happen, and paid to get it. That was what I found hardest to accept: that my opinion did not count in the slightest.

There was very little light, but it was enough to see the excitement on Alberto's face. I felt the exact opposite.

'Why don't we get out and go to bed together?' I suggested all at once, standing up and wiping the foam off my arms.

'OK! But just so long as you let me have some Colombian salsa,' he replied, standing up in the jacuzzi.

'Salsa?'

'Yes, that's right.'

'Of course! Do you want to dance?'

'No!'

'Ah . . .!' I said, and before he could say anything more, I wrapped myself in a towel and went off in search of Susana and a salsa CD.

It only took her a few seconds to put me straight. So I had been in the brothel less than an hour, and here I was with a client who had been with everyone in Barcelona and who was a complete cocaine addict.

I have never been attracted to drugs of any sort, although when I worked in the publicity agency, I saw people using them every day.

Susana put on some music anyway, and I went back into the room and lay down on the bed with Alberto. As was to happen often in my time in the brothel, we didn't even bother to draw back the bedcover. Alberto started to sniff his lines of coke and finished off the whisky Susana had served him when he arrived. That's quite an explosive mixture! I thought rather anxiously. Alberto's eyes took on a lost look, and he lay motionless on top of the cover.

A short while later he told me to get to work, but as he didn't even have the suspicion of an erection, I couldn't get the condom on him. I was quite clear in my own mind: there was no way I was going to do anything with a stranger without one.

'They'll be no use,' he told me, staring at the condoms I had put on the bedside table. 'I don't go for fucking. I only want you to give me a blow job, so there's no risk.'

202

'Let's see what we can do,' I said awkwardly.

I vanished for a moment into the next-door bathroom, saying I needed to pee urgently. I had a condom hidden in my hand, and when I got inside I took it out of its wrapper and put it on the tip of my tongue. I gently wet it with my saliva to warm the rubber up a bit, being very careful not to split it with my teeth. All at once it felt as though I had been doing this all my life. My brain was racing, trying to find an answer to the problem of protection. I didn't want to have an argument with my very first client. That wouldn't be a very good start to my career. I was hoping against hope he would not notice my little subterfuge.

He started shouting my name, and I hurried back into the bedroom. I was not looking forward to spending almost two hours more with a guy like him.

'What were you up to? Time's passing, and I paid for your services,' he reminded me reproachfully.

I didn't dare say anything in case he realized what I had in my mouth, so I just smiled back at him. He calmed down.

I spent all the rest of the two hours hard at work, but he never even guessed what was between my lips. It works, it works! I told myself, pleased at my spur-of-the-moment invention.

When his time was up, Alberto left just as he had come: out of his head on coke, and without ever having had a proper erection. But I had fifty thousand pesetas in my pocket, just like that!

'What do you do?' the brothel owner asked me, biro in one hand and notebook where she had written my name in the other.

We were in the kitchen, because there was a client in the small bedroom, and Susana was cleaning the suite.

'What do you mean?' I asked, realizing at once how stupid I was being.

'Do you have sex with men, with women? French style? Threesomes? Greek? I need to know. The more things you can offer, the more work you'll get.'

'Oh, I see ... well, with women I have no problem. French style, I always use a condom. And I don't do Greek.'

'That's a shame! Greek pays twice as much. A hundred thousand an hour. Fifty thousand for you. What about threesomes?'

'Threesomes?'

'Yes, when the client wants two girls.'

'Is that what you call it?'

'Yes, when the client wants two girls from the same brothel. It's less work because there are two of you.'

'I don't have a problem with that either. But I don't know any of the other girls yet. I suppose it's better to be with a girl you get on with, isn't it?'

'Of course. Though sometimes you don't get the choice. As far as working hours go, there are several possibilities. You can work day or night. Or if you prefer, you can be on call all the time. If you work at night, you have to be here before midnight, otherwise Susana won't open the door. During the day, we start at eight. If you want to be on call twenty-four hours, you can come whenever you want, but when you're not here, you should leave your mobile on so we can call you. That means you need to be always available. If we call you for a client and you can't come, we'll find another girl and know that in future we can't count on you.'

'I understand. That's normal.'

'If you need any days off, you just have to tell us.'

'OK. And what about when I have my period?'

Our conversation was interrupted by the appearance of a dark girl who swept into the kitchen dressed only in a tiny towel, revealing a fascinating glimpse of her pert buttocks.

'Cristina, the client says he wants some different music.'

'All right, Isa. I'll put another CD on.'

Isa was stunning, though a lot of it was silicone. I could tell from the way she looked at me what she thought of me: 'if looks could kill'. I introduced myself.

'Hello, I'm new here. My name is Val.'

Isa turned her head contemptuously and swept back out of the kitchen without so much as a word.

'Don't pay any attention,' the owner advised me. 'Most of the girls behave like that at first. Especially Isa. Every time someone new arrives, she gets like that. She seems them as competition. She's all right really. And she'll get used to you.' Then she added, 'Well, back to business. What times do you want to work?'

'Twenty-four hours,' I replied without hesitation.

'Good. That way you'll earn more money,' she said, jotting it down in her notebook without looking up.

'So what do I do now?' I wanted to know.

'You can stay if you like, or go home. But the girls here take preference. If a client arrives, we offer him the choice among them. It's only if he doesn't fancy any of them that we call the ones outside. We have a photobook to show the clients so they can choose the one they want. Do you have any photos of you we could use?'

'Not with me. But I'll have a look. What kind do you need?'

'Artistic ones. Your face, your body. But they have to be tasteful, we don't want anything vulgar. We're a top-class agency, remember.'

'Of course. But I don't think I have any photos like that.'

'All right, but if you want to work with us and don't want to waste any time, you should get together a photobook using a professional photographer.'

'OK!'

'Do you have one?'

'One what?'

'Do you have or know of a professional photographer?' asked Cristina patiently.

'No, but I can find one.'

'Good. But just so you know, we work with a very professional kid who also does our website, if you want to use him.'

'Oh, you do?'

I was surprised at how well organized they were.

'Yes. Whenever a new girl arrives, he takes care of their photobook. It takes a whole day, outside Barcelona. I would go with you to supervise things.'

'That sounds like a great idea. How much does a book cost, and how many photos do I need?'

'A good book costs around a hundred and twenty thousand pesetas, but to you it would be ninety thousand. There are twenty photos in it.'

She said the amount as if it were small change.

'Don't you think that's a bit expensive?' I asked, horrified at the cost.

'It's not much for a set of artistic photos,' Cristina said bluntly.

'I don't have any idea of the price of that kind of thing.'

'Well, photobooks are really expensive, believe me. But it's useful for your work. It's absolutely necessary, in fact.'

'All right. I'll do it, but let me work for a while first so I can save enough money, then we can organize the photo session,' I said thoughtfully.

'Of course. So, would you like to work a shift as well? Day or night?'

'At night, but I'll have my mobile on twenty-four hours a day as well, so you'll be able to call me at any time when I'm not here.'

'Fine. I can count on you then?'

'Yes, you can. Today I need to go home though. But I'll keep my phone on, so you can call me.'

'Good. Oh, by the way, at night you'll meet another manager. Her name is Angelika. She's a foreigner, but she speaks perfect Spanish. I'll tell her about you. A piece of advice: never tell a client or any of the other girls here that this is the first time you've done this sort of thing. Nobody will believe you. And one last thing: today you didn't do it because you didn't know, but after you've been in a bedroom with a client, you have to change the sheets straight away. Susana will look after the rest. Come with me and I'll show you where we keep the clean sheets. And the towels.'

We left the kitchen just as Susana came in, carrying the sheets from the bed I had been in with Alberto.

In the entrance to the apartment Cristina opened a large wooden wardrobe. Inside I could see a huge pile of sheets in one corner, and in the other stacks of clean towels for each girl to take as she needed. I noticed Susana was standing behind us. For some reason she had followed us from the kitchen, with her everlasting cigarette still stuck between her teeth. There was another wardrobe in the corridor, out of which dangled the strap of one of the girls' nightdresses. Cristina noticed what I was looking at.

'You can put your clothes in there. But be careful! You might not think it, but a lot gets stolen.'

'The girls steal from each other?' I said, taken aback.

Susana nodded. We all went back to the kitchen, and Cristina showed me how the coffee machine worked.

'There's coffee, tea, or chocolate. Just ask Susana. Each drink is a hundred and fifty pesetas. All right?'

'All right.'

Of course, everything here had to be paid for. And I had to change my own sheets! I said goodbye to Cristina and Susana, and went out into the street. I was pleased to have made fifty thousand pesetas for two hours' work, and told myself I was going to do as much as I could there. And despite my nerves before I had to attend my first client, I felt as if I had been doing this kind of thing all my life.

Miss Sarajevo

The night of 1st September 1999

Three in the morning.

It took me a long time to react: my mobile had been ringing for ages.

'Yes, hello?' I said, more dead than alive.

'Hello there Val, this is Angelika, the night manager at the brothel,' a very friendly voice said at the far end of the line. 'Were you asleep? I've been trying to get through for the past ten minutes.'

'Oh, hi! Yes, I was asleep, but it doesn't matter,' I said, sitting up. The word 'brothel' had woken me up properly. I didn't want to lose a single opportunity to work.

'Listen, I've got a job for you. He's a very good client. An Australian. He'll be expecting you at his place in twenty minutes. He'll pay fifty thousand plus the taxi, and if he likes you, he'll use you every week.'

'Fantastic! Where does he live?' I asked, searching for a biro.

'Write it down.'

While she was giving me his address, I was thinking about what I should wear.

'When you get there and he's paid you, call me. And call me again when you leave his place. Then come straight here with the money, right?'

'Yes, no problem,' I replied. 'What's the client's name?'

For some reason, this information seemed vitally important to me.

'David,' Angelika said, and hung up.

She sounded very friendly and professional. I was anxious to meet her.

I had a quick shower, called a taxi, and within fifteen minutes I was on my way to David's apartment.

The block was on the heights above Barcelona. A lovely place.

'Come up,' his voice said, and the entryphone echoed along the deserted street.

I found myself face to face with a very young guy. He was small, and wore a pair of round glasses that gave him an intellectual appearance. He wasn't particularly good-looking, but he seemed pleasant and sensitive. He smiled and invited me in. The flat was nice, but there wasn't much furniture, so I guessed he was a bachelor who had neither the time nor the inclination to do it up.

'Are you new?' he asked, after getting me to sit next to him on a blue sofa.

'Yes,' I said, smiling back at him. 'You can tell, can't you?'

'No, it's not that. It's just that I phone your agency every week, and I've never seen you before. That was why I thought you must be new. How long have you been working there?'

'Only since this afternoon,' I said, glancing at his bookshelves, full of books and CDs.

'Angelika told me you were French. I can see that just from looking at you,' he said, laughing.

'Yes, I am. And you're Australian, aren't you? You speak very good Spanish,' I replied, as he got up to look for something.

'We can speak French if you like. I studied it for years, although sometimes my vocabulary is a bit lacking,' he said, with another little laugh.

I laughed with him. He seemed really nice, even if he was a bit short for my liking.

He put the fifty thousand pesetas on the living-room table and suggested I count them.

'Now ring your agency and tell them everything is fine. If you don't you could be in trouble.'

'I see you know how it works,' I said, dialling the agency on my mobile.

Angelika replied at once.

'Everything OK?' she asked, as if she had just been waiting by the phone to hear from me.

'Yes, everything's fine.'

'Perfect. You have one hour. When you leave, ring to tell me you've finished.'

David showed me to his bedroom, and from that moment on, did not speak to me. I preferred it like that, as I didn't have much to say to him either. He started to undress me, and I was surprised at how skilfully he did it. I always imagined that men who paid to be with a girl could never make love properly, and were clumsy when they caressed you. But I was wrong, because David was not like that at all, so I decided to let myself go and forget the reason why I was there.

He kissed me all over my body, my buttocks, and my feet, then moved up suddenly and gently bit the back of my neck, before starting to move down me once more.

I found he had a tiny body, with a prick to match. But I didn't care. He was giving me a really good time.

There was a bottle of massage oil on his bedside table, and when he saw me looking at it he picked it up, still without a word, turned me over on my stomach, and began to massage my back. It was fantastic. He had the hands of a real professional. It was such a heavenly sensation I wouldn't mind being woken at three every night to be there with him like this.

I came round an hour later. I had red blotches all over my body, and he woke me with a gentle kiss on the lips. As I rode down in the lift, I felt as though I were floating. And on top of it all, I had been paid! I could hardly credit it.

I called Angelika as agreed, and found a taxi. In a quarter of an hour I was at the agency. It was a real pleasure to drive through Barcelona at that time of night, when it was completely empty. When I arrived, Angelika came down to open the street door for me. It's normally kept locked for security reasons.

She whispered a greeting so as not to wake the neighbours, and showed me up.

Angelika is an extraordinary woman. She is tall, with bright red hair, big blue eyes, and milky-white skin. No one would think she manages a brothel. The only thing I didn't like about her was that she looked too masculine for my taste.

We reached the apartment and went straight to the kitchen.

'There's a client in the suite, and the girls are sleeping in the other bedroom,' she explained.

To my surprise, she kissed me on both cheeks.

'I'm Angelika! Welcome!'

I found all this a bit exaggerated: after all, this was the first time we had met.

'Have you got the money?' she asked, opening a notebook with all the girls' names written in it, the times they had worked, and the amounts paid.

'Yes, here's your fifty thousand.'

'Thanks. And here's your twenty-five.'

She put a cross next to my name in the book.

'How was it with David?' she asked, obviously amused at the pink blotches on my face.

'Good, as you can see. He's a sweetheart; he needs a lot of affection.'

'Yes. All the girls are delighted when they know they're going to see him. If only they were all like him . . . Would you like a drink? I'll pay.'

'I could do with a coffee. I can scarcely keep my eyes open,' I said, yawning.

Angelika made me a coffee in the machine, then prepared herself a hot chocolate.

'Thanks,' I said, blowing on my coffee to cool it.

'Cristina told me you're going to work all round the clock. You'll earn lots of money that way. When are you going to be here?'

'At night, I think, I'm not sure, I imagine it depends on

how many clients there are, doesn't it?'

'That depends on which day it is. Some days there's more work in the daytime; others, it gets busy at night. But if you always keep your mobile on, you'll get plenty of work, you'll see.'

'How many girls work for the agency?' I was curious to know.

'Lots, though they don't all come here. Some of them just leave their photobook, and we only call them if no girl is available. To give you some idea, tonight six came for the night shift.'

When she said that, I realized how privileged I had been. She could have sent any of the girls in the brothel to visit David. It was strange, because the place seemed empty: there was no noise, not a sound. They must all have been asleep in the next room.

'Won't the others be upset it was me who went to David's?'

'Don't worry. He always wants someone new. He's been with all the girls here tonight already. Anyway, how are they to know?'

'I won't worry then.'

'What would you like to do? Stay here, or go home and start the night shift tomorrow?'

'I prefer to go home. I have to get used to this new rhythm.'

'Just as you like.'

'Thank you, Angelika.'

After I had said goodbye and got into a taxi, I realized a new day was dawning. I love the first light in the city. The air was clear and fresh, and I was so happy that I was noticing small things like that again. It had been a long time since I had enjoyed such a peaceful moment. Not only that, but in less than twenty-four hours I had earned seventy-five thousand pesetas, and I had really enjoyed myself with David. If only things carry on like this!

Careful, We're Being Watched!

2nd September 1999

I slept most of the morning. When I woke up, I wanted to go to the brothel as quickly as possible, to see if there was any work. But I stayed at home, and there wasn't a single call all day.

I finally went to the agency at around half past eleven in the evening, as Cristina had recommended, with a bag of nightwear. The downstairs door was still open, so I went straight up to the apartment. Susana showed me in.

'Hello there, sweetheart! You're early. Most of the girls working at night get here just before twelve, five minutes before the shift starts. You'll do the same, I'm sure, once you've got used to it,' Susana commented, her big round eyes fixed on me.

'Cristina said that if I wasn't here before twelve, I wouldn't be able to get in.'

'Yes, that's the rule.' Then she added, changing topics, 'Some of the girls from the day shift are still here. They'll be leaving soon, and so will I. Let me introduce you to them.'

The rule! It made this sound like a convent!

We went into the living room (meaning there were no clients, otherwise the door would have been shut, because it gives directly onto the suite). I could hear voices and, from time to time, the sound of laughter.

Three girls were sitting on the sofa, and one on the floor. I was surprised at how different they all were. I recognized Isa, the mulatto who had refused to say hello yesterday. She had a big head of hair, fleshy lips, and a tiny nose that had obviously been operated on. She was wearing a light suede outfit that brought out the cinnamon colour of her skin. Her plunging neckline revealed a pair of enormous breasts – thirty-eight at least – that had also been under the surgeon's knife, as another of the girls wickedly told me later on. Bit by bit, I managed to win Isa over, and we even had some surreal conversations about how crazy people are.

'Everybody's mad, you know,' she would constantly tell me. 'All mad. And especially men! They're off their heads! They must be crazy to pay a woman for a fuck!'

In fact, this was about the limit of her conversation. She never talked about anything else, but she did make me laugh a lot, although at the same time I couldn't help feeling sorry for her.

Whatever money she earned, she spent on clothes. One day after she had worked hard, she splashed out a hundred and fifty thousand pesetas on new rags. She would tell everyone she was twenty-nine, even though she had seen at least forty-two summers: all her operations kept her looking young. She was the eldest of all of us, and she thought this gave her more rights, which was why she always scowled at any newcomer.

Today I was the new girl, so she hardly deigned to look at me. After what had happened yesterday, I wasn't surprised.

Next to her was a tall, gorgeous redhead, with long straight hair down to her hips. I thought at first that Estefania was Swedish. Later I was told she was Spanish, from Valladolid! She said nothing about the fact that I had borrowed her red dress to see my first client. Cristina must have smoothed things over. Estefania had an angelic face, with soft, big blue eyes. She was working as a prostitute to keep a much older man, who did nothing himself because he couldn't be bothered. I never found out much more about her, because she was always very discreet, and rarely talked about herself. Tonight, she greeted me with a smile. Over time, I came to think she was the smartest of them all: she only spoke when necessary, otherwise she simply smiled. It was she who taught me that talking in a place like that was the worst thing you could do.

Mae was Spanish as well, but from Asturias. She had short blonde hair, and long legs. She was very attractive, but mistrust oozed from her every pore. I immediately sensed I would have to be careful with her, because I could see she was a real snake. She was always boasting about she had been a model, but clearly she hadn't made a great success of it . . . She had a lot of admirers, and obviously lived off men, both inside and outside the brothel. She would disappear for weeks on end, whenever she had a new man in her life. Once the money and the relationship were exhausted, she would reappear like a stray dog. She gave herself airs, but in my opinion she was the most common of them all.

Cindy, a black-eyed Portuguese girl, was the only one who spoke to me when I came into the room. She was the witch who had arranged for the lemon and cigarette to be burning in the entrance hall. She had shiny raven-black hair, and a muscular body.

'Hi there! You're French, aren't you?' she asked.

'Yes. I'm Val.'

'Pleased to meet you,' she said, shaking my hand.

This formal politeness was in sharp contrast not only to her surroundings, but to the vulgar dress she was wearing. I put it down to the fact that she did not know much Spanish. In fact, as I learned, her Spanish was dreadful: she was always mixing it up with Portuguese. So she would come out with the few stock phrases she knew, and mix that with the worst kind of slang, making me think she must once have been a streetwalker. I knew immediately though that she would be my friend, and we always got on very well. Cindy worked on both the day and the night shifts, because she had serious problems with money.

'I have a *filha* to bring up, for fuck's sake,' she would tell me all the time.

Whenever I heard her, I burst out laughing. She considered herself such a lady, but could not stop herself talking that way. She was completely surrealist too.

So I had now met the four most established girls in the brothel. Susana motioned to me to follow her back into the kitchen.

'Listen, sweetheart, make sure you don't get into a fight with any of them. There are always problems between them, but don't get involved. I'm telling you for your own good,' insisted Susana, as if I were about to contradict her, 'you'll thank me for it some day, you'll see! And if anything does happen, come and talk to me or Cristina about it. She's the boss.'

'Fine,' I said, without hesitation.

All at once we heard shrieks from the living room.

It was Isa.

'I bet one of you whores has stolen my Versace jacket!' she shouted hysterically.

'One of us?' Mae shouted back. 'You're the crazy whore around here. I can buy all the Versace jackets I want, you idiot.'

'You can, can you? So how come my jacket has vanished since you arrived?'

Susana ran out of the kitchen.

'What's going on here?' she asked, a lit cigarette in her hand as ever.

'Someone has stolen my Versace jacket,' Isa told her. 'And I bet it was one of them.'

I looked on, clutching my plastic bag of clothes tightly, in case a robber leapt out of the wardrobe.

Just then, the electric intercom sounded.

'A client! All of you, go to the bedroom and put some make-up on! That's enough squabbling!' said Susana. She turned to me. 'You too, Val.'

We all ran into the small bedroom to change. We were taking our work clothes out of our bags, when I saw Isa staring at mine. I knew immediately what she was thinking.

'Let's see your bag,' she said aggressively.

'My bag?' I said, bridling. 'Why do you want to look there? You surely don't think I . . . ?'

She snatched it from me and emptied the contents onto the bed.

'You can't do that!' I shouted.

'If it wasn't one of you, who else could it be?' she asked, certain she was going to find her jacket among my things.

But it wasn't there.

'See? I didn't take it!'

'Come off it,' said Cindy. 'How could you imagine that this poor girl, who's only just arrived, could have stolen your jacket?'

'I didn't ask for your opinion,' Isa exploded, throwing the plastic bag back at me. 'And anyway, she hasn't just arrived. She stole a client from me yesterday afternoon.'

I really thought I must be dreaming. I wanted to defend myself, but Cindy responded before I could even open my mouth.

'What are you talking about?' she raged. 'You think the clients are yours? For fuck's sake! The clients come to the brothel, Isa, they don't belong to you!'

I began to feel terrible with all this going on.

'The problem is,' Isa retorted, 'that there are too many hens in this hen house.'

'Of course,' Mae butted in, furious as well. 'You'd like to be the only one working here. That's IMPOSSIBLE . . . get it, big silicone tits? We've got just as much right to be here as you have.'

'I prefer having silicone breasts to droopy ones like you, fat ass,' Isa snapped, to put an end to the argument.

I was afraid they were going to attack each other physically, but at that moment Susana came in to sort things out.

'What are you doing? You can hear the noise out in the street. Come on, get ready because there's a client and he wants to see all of you.'

I had decided to put on a black Chinese outfit for work that night. A really smart pair of trousers and blouse. Not too vulgar, but not too sophisticated either. Perfect, I thought. But I still had no idea how I was supposed to behave in front of a client, and I was upset at the row I had just witnessed.

'Relax!' said Cindy, who had obviously recovered much more quickly than me. 'The client isn't going to eat you.'

Isa was the first to go into the room. She strode in haughtily like a diva. She soon came out, and I was the next in. I found myself confronted by a youngster with a spotty face, who was obviously uncomfortable. I smiled at him.

'Hello, I'm Val, and I'm French,' I said, holding out my hand like an idiot.

The boy didn't even look at me, and I knew at once he wasn't going to choose me.

After we had all been into the room, and then learnt that he had chosen Estefania, Cindy asked me how I had gone about introducing myself.

'God, no wonder he didn't pick you!' she laughed. 'You have to seduce the client. Kiss him on both cheeks, don't give him your fucking hand.'

'Aha?'

'Yes, otherwise he'll get scared. You have to sell yourself. Oh, and don't wear trousers. Put a skirt on, and the shorter the better.'

It was odd. Whenever I have met someone in the street

or elsewhere who I've wanted, I've never had any problem getting him into bed. But here, everything was different. To start with there were other girls, so obviously I had competition. But also, I felt inhibited. I didn't dare let myself go.

'If you want to do this and earn money, you have to be the best f . . . of all,' Cindy added. I was surprised she didn't say the word full out.

'What are you doing, giving her advice?' Mae snapped as she took her make-up off. 'Let her find out for herself! This job is hard enough without you teaching any newcomer the tricks of the trade so she can steal our clients.'

Cindy pretended not to hear, and turned to me.

'Does what I said make sense?'

'Yes, Cindy. And thanks.'

'It's my pleasure.'

She lay down on the bed, while Mae picked up her things and left, without saying goodbye. That left just three of us: Cindy, Isa and me. I decided to sleep for a while. Although I had not done anything, I felt exhausted.

The three of us were trying to sleep uncomfortably in the same bed, when Angelika flung open the door. I woke with a start: I'd been fast asleep.

'Isa, get up will you? You have a client in a hotel in twenty minutes. I've already called you a taxi, so get a move on!'

With that she shut the door again, and Isa began to get ready. It's bad enough being awakened in the middle of the night, but it's much worse if you have to get up, put on make-up, and get dressed carefully. But Isa did not say a word. I looked at my watch: three in the morning.

Good God! Who on earth could want a girl at this time of night? I looked round and saw that Cindy was still fast asleep, snoring like a dormouse. There was no sign of Estefania. She must still be with the same client in the suite. As Isa finished getting ready, I decided to get up too, because I was sure I wouldn't be able to go back to sleep. Instead, I went out into the kitchen in my pyjamas to talk to Angelika.

'Hello, Angelika,' I greeted her hoarsely.

She was painting her nails.

'Hello! What's up? Can't you sleep? How did you get on tonight?' she asked, raising her head for a few seconds before concentrating on her fingernails once more.

'Nothing doing,' I said. 'Nothing at all!'

'Don't worry, you'll see – as soon as you go back to bed, the phone will ring. That's always the way. Work always comes when you least expect it. It's hard to plan anything,' she continued, twisting her mouth in distaste.

Isa appeared in the doorway, done up to the nines. Just then, the taxi-driver called on the intercom.

'Here's the address. Princesa Sofia Hotel. Room 237. Mister Peter. Call me as soon as you get there.'

Isa took the piece of paper Angelika held out to her, and left without a word.

'She's a bit odd, don't you think?' Angelika said to me.

'Yes, she's already caused trouble tonight.'

'Yes, Susana told me. Oh well, she has her problems. Did you know she's got two children back in Ecuador?'

'She has?' I said, stupefied.

'Yes, but she never sees them. I don't get it. She's the one who gets most work here, she earns a fortune, and yet she doesn't want to bring her children to Spain. As a mother, I just can't understand her.'

'You've got children too?'

Her face lit up.

'I've got a wonderful boy,' she said. 'What about you?'

'No, not yet.'

'So you're not doing this because you have a child to support? Good for you!'

I was surprised she didn't go on to ask why it was I had started at the brothel. I felt almost obliged to explain myself, but before I could do so, Estefania appeared in the doorway. Her eyeliner was smudged, and she looked as if all she wanted to do was sleep.

'He's paying for another hour. Here's the money,' she told Angelika.

'That's great! You're making a real night of it.'

'Yes, but I'm getting pretty fed up with it as well.'

With that, she turned on her heel and left.

'She does a lot, doesn't she?' I said.

'She and Isa are the two busiest. She spends all the time here between Tuesday and Friday. It's dreadful, isn't it?' Angelika said, visibly upset by the idea. Then she asked, 'And do you know what the worst of it is?'

'No.'

'She does it to keep a guy who spends the whole day doing nothing.'

'I don't understand. Is he her pimp?'

'If she works here and he lives off her, I guess you could call him that,' said Angelika, horrified.

'Well, we've all helped a man at some point in our lives,' I replied, remembering my own personal drama.

'Well, I haven't, that's for sure! When I see the poor

girls here working like crazy selling their bodies, I think it's only right they spend all the money they earn on themselves, don't you?' She checked herself when she realized she had raised her voice. 'I must speak more softly, the walls here have ears.'

'What do you mean?' I asked.

'The owners,' Angelika replied, this time almost whispering.

'The owners? What do you mean? That they have microphones and record all we say?' I said, almost laughing out loud.

I was sure she was joking, but Angelika suddenly looked apprehensive and put a finger to my lips.

'Shhh! They might hear you. And yes,' she said, still in a whisper, 'there are microphones everywhere, except here in the kitchen. They also record all the phone calls.'

'What are you saying?' I asked, terrified.

'It's true,' she replied. 'Haven't any of the girls said anything to you? It's to make sure none of them give their phone numbers to clients. And the phone line is tapped so the owners can check Susana and I are doing our job properly. Like something out of a film, isn't it?'

'It's worse!' I protested. 'It's wrong; it's a violation of people's privacy! How dare they keep tabs on us like that? Besides, if a girl wants to give a client her phone number, how are they going to stop her?'

'I agree,' said Angelika. 'If you go to a hotel to see a client, you can do as you like. But you have to be very careful with the owner, Manolo. His wife Cristina is lovely, but he . . .'

'I haven't met him yet.'

'He's awful! He looks like your typical lorry driver. I

226

call him a Neanderthal, if you know what I mean. He's vulgar and super aggressive. You'll meet him soon enough. They play a double game: he's the one who gets angry; she's the one who comforts people. They control all the girls as though they were their parents.'

So at last I'd found the famous lorry-driver pimp I was dreaming of! And Neanderthal as well! That sounded promising.

'You'll have plenty of time to find out everything I'm telling you is true. But please, don't tell anyone it was me who told you, OK?' Angelika almost begged me. 'I don't want to lose this job. I've got money worries, and although I do a few things in the daytime, this is what I live off.'

'Of course I won't say anything. Now I'm going back to bed, all of a sudden I feel really tired.'

'Just one other thing,' Angelika said, a serious look on her face. 'Don't trust Susana, the day manager. She's crazy too.'

'All right, I won't. Thanks for the warning,' I said, yawning and not paying too much attention to what she was saying.

So I went back to the bedroom, wondering why Angelika had been so open with me when she hardly knew me. It all seemed very strange, but one thing was plain: there was a lot going on, and I had to be careful. Manolo, the microphones, Susana . . . It all sounded like some TV soap opera. Then again, I couldn't ask for too much. After all, this was a brothel. And besides, it all helped boost my adrenalin. For the first time in a long while, something was happening to me that I had chosen. And that's what is best of all.

I opened the bedroom door as carefully as possible so as not to disturb Cindy. But she was in exactly the same position as before: lying on her side, sleeping like a baby. I reckoned nothing would wake her. I got into bed as well, and went back to sleep until all of a sudden Angelika came in again. Like before, she switched the light on and I woke up.

'Hey, do you speak English?' she asked, shaking me by the shoulder.

'Yes, very well.'

'Hurry and get up then. I've got a client in the Juan Carlos Hotel who wants a European girl who speaks English.'

It was awful having to wake up again. But it was worse still trying to make myself up. How on earth was I going to get rid of the dark circles under my eyes? I was beginning to find it much less fun. And this was only the first night I had spent in the brothel!

'I'll call a taxi. Come on, hurry up!' Angelika insisted. 'Here are the details of your client. He's called Sam, he's in room 315. He's paying sixty thousand for an hour.'

When she heard the price, Cindy lifted her head a few inches, and then she wished me 'Good luck!' and fell back to sleep again. So that was what it took to rouse her: the mention of money. Estefania was sleeping alongside her. I hadn't even heard her come into the room. She was already fast asleep, and had not even stirred. How many girls could fit into the bed? Later on, we got five of us into it. A world record!

It was five in the morning. Any client who wanted a girl at that time must be really starved.

I went downstairs as quietly as I could, and was

228

annoyed to find the taxi had not yet arrived. Several drunks appeared out of a striptease club and tried to attract my attention, but I ignored them. I felt a huge gulf between them and me. I felt important: I was going to have sex with someone who was paying sixty thousand pesetas for the privilege, in a luxury hotel. A five-star hotel. And with a bit of luck, I was even going to enjoy myself. When I realized what I was thinking, I felt ridiculous. It was all a question of price.

The taxi-driver finally arrived. As soon as I told him the address, he realized why I was going. I could see him looking at me in the rear-view mirror, trying to strike up a conversation. But all I did was smile back at him, and say nothing.

When I got to the hotel, I walked straight to the lifts as purposefully as I could. I avoided looking at the receptionists, so that they would not ask me anything. I wanted to look like a guest. It worked. Nobody stopped me, and I was soon on my way to the third floor.

When the client opened the door, I found myself facing a very tall dark-skinned man. He looked Indian, and his sharp Asian features attracted me at once. The white bathrobe he was wearing gave him an endearing, friendly appearance.

'Hello, are you Sam?' I asked, responding to his welcoming smile.

'Yes, you must be the girl from the agency.'

'Yes. My name is Val. Pleased to meet you.'

He showed me in. My money was already on the bed-side table.

'You can take it,' he said. 'It's yours!'

'OK. Thank you,' I replied. 'Can I call my agency to say that everything is OK?'

'Yes of course,' he said, disappearing into the bathroom.

I called Angelika, then began to undress. Sam reappeared, and said I could use the bathroom if I wanted to. I thanked him for that too, while he served himself some red wine from the minibar.

I spent a very pleasant hour with him. He was very sweet, and although I didn't have an orgasm, I enjoyed myself. He was very good at caressing me. Afterwards, he gave me a twenty-thousand-peseta tip and presented me with his business card, should I ever need anything. He promised to ask for me whenever he was in Barcelona. I had to rush out, because Angelika called to say the hour was up. I had completely forgotten about the time.

'I'm not bothered,' Angelika told me, 'but if you do that with Susana, she'll really cause problems. So make sure you watch the time. Otherwise, they'll think you're being paid more and are only giving them the fee for an hour, right?'

It was seven o'clock by the time I got back to the agency. I paid Angelika, but said nothing about the tip or my client's business card. Then I went straight back to bed.

Manolo The Lorry Driver

3rd September 1999

Nine in the morning.

I was woken by terrible noise and the sound of some madman shouting at the top of his voice. I was alone in the bed, and there was a pile of crumpled sheets in one corner. I got up and went straight to the kitchen to make myself a coffee. I ran into a stocky dark-haired man in shorts, a bumbag that was full to bursting around his waist. He was wearing a pair of loafers that made a strange contrast with his shorts. His bottle-green tee shirt had 'I Love Nicaragua' written on it. He looked furious, and Susana, who was with him, was as red as a tomato. He stared at me hard for a few moments, as if I were disturbing them.

I did not know who he was, but from the crass way he was dressed and the violence all too obvious on his face, I guessed this must be Manolo, the brothel owner. He was exactly as Angelika had described him. It seemed I was the only girl left in the apartment, and I felt a sudden stab of fear at being alone with someone like him. All the girls had vanished into thin air.

'So who are you?' Manolo said, breaking the ice as only he could.

'Hello, I'm Val. I'm new here. I only started two days ago.'

'Oh, yes! My wife told me there was a new girl. Hello, I'm Manolo,' he said, shaking my hand roughly.

He did not look me in the face when I took his hand. He seemed preoccupied with something else. And he immediately launched into, 'I was just telling this idiot Susana here that I don't want any more fights between the girls. She's the manager, and has to sort things out, right?'

What was he doing, asking me for my opinion in front of Susana? I didn't think that was very proper, but how on earth was I going to tell a Neanderthal like him what I thought? So all I did was keep looking at him. In the few hours I'd been working in the agency, I had realized that you get work if the manager is on your side. If I fell out with Susana, I was sure she would never call me for a client during her day shift.

'Did you hear me, idiot? I've had it up to here with the girls phoning me at home to complain. Either you do your job or you're out in the fuckin' street!'

How vulgar could you get? I couldn't understand someone like Manolo. Why do people like him always have to conform exactly to the stereotype of the vulgar, violent pimp? If Susana really is crazy, as Angelika claimed, I could see why. With a boss like this guy, anyone's brain would be affected.

From that moment on, I promised myself to be as

bland as possible whenever Manolo was around, to avoid his attitude becoming contagious.

I made my coffee, paid Susana her 150 pesetas, and went to the living room to get some peace and quiet. All of a sudden there was a loud hammering noise from the floor below, and Manolo rushed furiously out of the kitchen. It really was so loud it would have driven anyone mad.

'They're going to destroy the whole fuckin' building if they carry on like that!' shouted Manolo.

Susana followed at his heel like a little dog, cigarette in hand. She had obviously forgotten how badly he had been treating her, and shadowed his every move.

'It's like this every day,' she explained.

'When the fuck are they going to finish all that building work? I'm going down to see how much longer they intend to take.'

'OK.'

Manolo turned to Susana and wagged a finger in her face.

'I want that to be the last time there's any fighting in here. Otherwise, you're out in the street, got it? In the fuckin' street . . .'

'Yes, Manolo,' Susana replied meekly.

Then he stared at me again, and gave a short wave of goodbye.

'Not exactly easy, is he?' I said to Susana, trying to be friendly.

'He can be difficult, but he's right. I shouldn't allow the girls to phone him at night to complain.'

She looked askance at me, as if I was the one she suspected. I could tell that, strangely enough, she wasn't mad at Manolo. With him, she was a complete masochist.

The doorbell rang. It was a client, and Susana showed him into the living room, while I ran with my cup of coffee to hide in the small bedroom. A few moments later Susana came in to tell me to get ready, because I was the only girl in the apartment.

'I can't see anyone like this, Susana. Have you seen how I look? I've got bags under my eyes, and I'm exhausted. I need to go home and rest.'

'Oh, sweetheart! What are you saying? I thought you wanted to work.'

'Of course I want to work. But when I feel up to it.'

'You should get dressed, put some make-up on, and see the client. It's up to him to decide if you're up to it or not.'

I didn't dare say a thing. Not because I was afraid of her – I had no problems telling her what I thought – but because I didn't want to start an argument. And it was true, I was there to work. So I got ready.

As I had thought, the client wasn't impressed by the way I looked. He greeted me, but then asked to see the photobook, because I wasn't what he wanted.

'You see, I told you so,' I said to Susana, putting on a pair of jeans.

'All right, you can go home. Estefania is going to come back. I called her. She was out having breakfast, but I'm sure the client will like her. I don't know what you've done to leave your face in such a state,' she said, glancing at me again in that furtive way of hers.

When I heard her comment, I could understand why the girls were so vain about their appearance, and were

234

always buying themselves stuff to put on, and spending the whole day in front of the mirror. Remarks like Susana's could easily depress you, send you rushing to a plastic surgeon, or leave your self-confidence at zero. Mine was already there anyway, so I tried to shrug her comment off, picked up my bag of things, and went home.

The Sponge

4th September 1999

I didn't go to work last night because my period started. I felt awful, and stayed in bed all day.

At eleven I got a call from the agency owner, Cristina. She wanted to know how I was, and when we could organize my photo session.

'I feel dizzy, Cristina. Not well at all. And I know I'll be like this for six days at least.'

'Six days?' she said. 'Does your period last that long?'

'Yes, unfortunately. But I think I should be able to do the photos in about three.'

'Good. I spoke to our photographer. He wants to go to the Costa Brava. It's very pretty there, and we could do some really elegant photos, if you agree.'

'Sounds great.'

'We'd have to leave early, around six in the morning, to take advantage of the light.'

'I understand. Six is a bit early for me, but that's fine. I want to get the photos done.'

'Why don't you call by the apartment this afternoon. That way we can organize the photo session, and we can talk about what you should wear. I'll be there around four.'

So I forced myself out of bed.

When I got to the brothel, there were more girls present than usual. They were all sitting in the living room, watching a soap on TV. Cindy, the Portuguese girl, was walking round the room with a lit stick of cinnamon.

'This attracts money,' she said when she saw me staring at her in amazement. 'Afterwards, I'm going into the kitchen to wave the cinnamon round the phone, so that clients will call.'

She seemed completely serious as she told me all this. I couldn't help laughing, but I stopped abruptly when I saw a blonde girl coming out of the bathroom. She looked just like a Barbie doll: the same tangled mass of hair, a tight-fitting tee shirt that showed off her huge silicone breasts and matching plump lips. Her breasts were so exaggerated I thought they were going to swallow her up completely. She had had such a severe facelift her eyes were completely expressionless. I thought her plastic surgeon had overdone it, to say the least. She was tiny, but round in all the right places. What on earth had she done to herself? She looked at me without saying anything, then went to sit next to Isa, who was busy putting on lipstick with the help of a small hand mirror. I could see at once the two of them were friends, and that was why the Barbie doll seemed to dislike me even before we had met. Isa must have already set her against me.

Cristina came out of the kitchen and called me.

'Come in here, it's easier to talk,' she said in a friendly way.

She was finding it hard to move around because she was eight months pregnant, but every time I saw her she seemed to be in a good mood.

'The blonde girl is called Sara. You haven't met her before, have you?'

'No, this is the first time I've seen her,' I said.

'She's worked for us for years. The men love her.'

'They do?'

I was disgusted, and thought yet again what little taste most men have.

'She can be a bit strange at first, but don't worry, she'll come round.'

To tell the truth, I didn't really care one way or the other. I was just taken aback because I had imagined there would be more friendship and solidarity among the girls. But I already realized I had been mistaken. I felt truly disappointed.

'Every morning when I wake up I think I'm about to explode,' Cristina said. 'I'm so fed up with this pregnancy. I just wish the baby would come . . . !'

'I can imagine,' I said. 'And it must be dreadful with this awful heat, isn't it?'

'Yes. And I've got no one to help me. I'm rushing about, and at home Manolo is a good man, but he's completely wrapped up in his own affairs. He doesn't do any chores for me. I've heard you've already met my husband, haven't you?'

'Yes. I met him yesterday morning. I looked ghastly because I was about to get my period, and that's how he saw me.'

'He shouts a lot, doesn't he?' she said, laughing. 'I've already told him, Manolo don't get so nervous. But he never listens. Oh . . .' She suddenly clutched her belly. 'I'm just the opposite, thank God! It doesn't do to blow your top in this job. There are always problems, and the only way to deal with them is to stay calm, don't you think?'

'I suppose so.'

'We have a clothes shop as well. Manolo and I run it. You should call in one day, we have some nice stuff. Perhaps you'll need to renew your wardrobe. I'll give you a special price.'

'Why not?'

'Anyway, to get back to business: how about doing the shoot the day after tomorrow? You'll have to bring some elegant dresses, some nightwear, your own make-up. We'll probably have to retouch the photos, because you're bound to sweat a lot in this heat,' Cristina went on, giving me the impression she knew all there was to know about these things. She changed topics. 'As far as your periods go, you're going to lose a lot of money if you're out of action six days a month.'

'Yes, I know, but what can I do about it?' I said wearily.

'There is something you can do so that you can work without your client realizing you have your period.'

'What's that?'

She had taken me by surprise. Every day in this place I learn something new. Cristina went on to give me all the details.

'Tricks of the trade, sweetheart. If you have a client, instead of using a tampon, use a nice big soft sea sponge.

Cut off a bit, otherwise it will be too big. While you're having sex, the client won't notice a thing.'

'Does it really work?' I asked, still only half-convinced.

'Of course it does! Try it and you'll see.'

This woman is determined to make sure I earn as much as possible.

'I'm telling you this because tonight there are two politicians from Madrid who want girls. I'm sending Cindy, and I think you'd be good too. They want girls they can be seen having a drink with. For the moment, they've paid for an hour just chatting, but nothing more. I'm sure though that if they get on with you, they'll take you back to their hotel.'

I thought it over for a minute, and decided it might be interesting. I would agree.

'All right. What time will it be?'

'At midnight. Only one of them knows you're being paid. It has to look like a chance meeting, as though you were a friend of his. His colleague is never to know all this has been set up, understand?'

'Yes, but how will it work?'

The whole thing seemed absurd to me.

'Manuel, our accomplice – to call him something – will arrive at the bar with his friend around midnight. He'll be wearing a grey suit, and a red Loewe tie. When you see him, you go up and ask if he remembers meeting you at such-and-such a place. Remember, you go up to him. Then he'll ask both of you to have a drink with them, and you sit with them. No problem!'

'All right, I'll make sure things go smoothly.'

'Good. Manuel has already seen Cindy's photo, and

I've told him about you. You speak Spanish better than she does, so it's up to you to set everything up. Your friend has just arrived from Lisbon, by the way.' She paused, then wrote an address on a piece of paper. 'Twelve midnight in this bar. Come here first to pick up Cindy, then the two of you go on there.'

'Got it.'

'And then the day after tomorrow, I'll see you at six in the morning, right?'

'Right.'

Politically Incorrect

The night of 4th September 1999

After talking to Cristina, I went home to sort out what I was going to wear that night and for the photoshoot the day after tomorrow. In the evening, I went back to the apartment. My whole body was tingling: I like this kind of chance meeting. It's really thrilling, it gives me an adrenalin rush, and makes me feel as though my head is going to explode from all the blood pounding at my temples.

Cindy was ready when I arrived, so we took a taxi to the bar. I was picturing what the two politicians might look like: very serious in their Ermenegildo Zegna suits, their pockets stuffed with notes and business cards, perhaps leather briefcases containing unpronounceable speeches written by others more skilled than them at constructing a coherent argument. I had never spoken to a real politician. What kind of language would Manuel use with me? We were supposed to talk for an hour: what could we say to each other?

'Do you know what this Manuel looks like?' Cindy asked all of a sudden, putting a stop to my inner monologue.

'I haven't the faintest idea!' I confessed. 'All I know is that he'll be wearing a grey suit and a red Loewe tie.'

'How are we supposed to know what a red Loewe tie looks like?' Cindy protested, smoothing down the hem of her skirt, which had ridden up when she got into the taxi. She kept lifting herself up to tug at the material stuck under her backside. As she did so, I got a glimpse of her stockings and the garter round the top. She looked very sexy tonight.

'I don't know. But we'll find them.'

The bar was up in Tibidabo, with a fantastic view over Barcelona. It was pretty dark inside, and the music was going full blast. Not exactly the ideal place to meet two politicians from Madrid. We were going to have to shout our heads off just to make ourselves heard!

I left Cindy on her own for a moment and went to the bathroom. I had my sponge in my bag. I was waiting until the very last minute to put it in. At home I had taken the trouble to cut it into three pieces, because the original ball was far too big. As soon as I was locked in the cubicle, I took out one of the pieces and carefully inserted it. It gave me a strange feeling to be doing this, but it was my only option. It also took me quite a while, because I was not used to it. Then I went back to join Cindy, who was closely studying every man who came in the bar. It was so dark inside that, like cats, all their suits looked grey, and I was beginning to think we were going to have a hard time finding our clients.

'Can you see anything?' Cindy asked me.

'No, not a thing. But it's not midnight yet. I don't expect they'll be punctual anyway. Let's wait a bit longer.'

We asked for a drink: Cindy wanted a gin and tonic, and I had a whisky and Coke. We began to chat. Cindy seemed very pleasant, with very clear ideas and a tremendous loathing for men that she made no attempt to hide.

'I can't stand them. Only for work; apart from that I don't want to know,' she said, raising her glass in a toast with me.

'Don't you have a boyfriend at least?'

'A boyfriend?' she almost shouted. 'You must be crazy! Just so that he can spy on me and discover everything I'm doing, then start a scandal? No, no, no . . . I had more than enough with the father of my *filha*.'

'What happened with him?'

'What happened was that when my girl was two years old, he left me for another woman. Since then, he hardly ever comes to see *sua filha* and gives me next to nothing for her keep. He's such an asshole! And he's got dough, the idiot! That's why I don't want a boyfriend. Besides, I wouldn't know how to be with a man who didn't pay me now.'

'Too bad!' I didn't know what else to say. 'But you're OK in the agency, aren't you?'

'Yes. Sometimes there's *muito trabajo*, and at others, nothing. But I always pick at something.'

'You pick at something?' I liked Cindy a lot, but I was having a hard time understanding her, what with the noise of the customers and the loud music, and the way she used Portuguese words and expressions the whole time.

'*Sim*. I mean I always find work. I used to work in New York and London, so I've been around. What about you? Why are you here?'

Even though I felt I could trust her, I did not want to go into detail about my life.

'A man's to blame for that too. He stole money from me, and I have debts.'

'I get it. So now it's you who makes the guys pay. It's your revenge.'

'I don't know. I don't think it's just that.'

As I was trying to explain to Cindy my reasons for joining the agency, I could feel someone caressing me with their eyes. Instinctively, I looked up, and saw a man whispering into his friend's ear. Two men on their own! It must be them! I couldn't make out the colour of his tie. It looked quite bright, but I couldn't swear it was red. But they were the only two men on their own at the bar, so without giving it a second thought, I left Cindy in mid-sentence and decided to go over to the man looking so intently at me. As I stood up, I could feel something wasn't right between my legs. The sponge had moved, and I felt tremendous stomach cramps, and as though my legs were made of cotton wool.

Cindy could tell something was wrong, and grabbed me by the arm.

'Are you feeling all right?' she asked, visibly disturbed.

'Yes, it's nothing. It's only the stupid sponge . . . Wait, I think I've seen them. Over there at the end of the bar. I'll be right back.'

I could feel beads of sweat on my brow, but I had stood up and was looking at them purposefully, so I had to go through with it. I did the best I could.

'Aren't you Manuel?' I asked, trying hard to raise a smile.

'No, I'm Antonio, and my friend here is Carlos. And what's your name, gorgeous?' said the guy who was supposed to be wearing a grey suit and a red tie.

When I heard their names, my face fell.

'Sorry, I thought you were someone else. I'm really sorry, I was sure you were him.'

I extricated myself as quickly as possible, before I was completely overcome with embarrassment. It had all been for nothing, and I had looked ridiculous walking over there, as if I were wearing a baby's nappy. By the time I got back to my seat, Cindy was deep in conversation with two men at the next table.

'They're from Kuwait,' she explained. 'But they only speak English, not a word of Spanish. I *falou* a *poquinho* of English, but it's hard. What about you?'

The two Kuwaits were eyeing me up and down in a way that left little doubt as to their intentions.

'Look, if our two guys don't show up, I'll pick up one of these Arabs. They've got money, and I'm sure they'd pay well. We could keep the lot, and not tell them a thing at the agency.'

'Are you crazy? Susana is expecting my call, and our clients haven't appeared. If they don't, we'll have to go straight back to the apartment.'

'Well, she can wait a bit, and besides, she's just about to leave and soon Angelika will be in charge. She's great: all we have to do is go back and tell her we waited and they never came. And in the meantime, we can have these two here.'

To her, it was all quite simple.

'Do you want something to drink?' one of the men suggested.

'No thanks. I'm sorry but we are waiting for some friends,' I replied, ultra-politely.

I was beginning to get anxious.

'I'm going to give them *meu* telephone,' said Cindy, searching in her bag for a pen to write her number down with.

'Don't hesitate to call me,' she said, handing one of them a piece of paper.

'Are you satisfied?' I said, almost angrily. 'Everybody is staring at us. Now we really do look like hookers.'

'Don't get so annoyed! You'll soon be doing exactly the same as me, you'll see! A man who looks at you means money in the bank, you can bet on it.'

She burst out laughing.

She may have been right, but as yet I didn't feel I could behave like that.

'Val?'

I turned round to see who was calling me. I found myself face to face with a man of around thirty-seven, wearing a grey suit with a red tie. Not only was he attractive, but I was impressed by his impeccable manners. I didn't think twice about it, but replied, 'Manuel? I don't believe it! What are you going here? I thought you lived in Madrid.'

He kissed me on both cheeks as though we were old friends.

'Let me get a proper look at you. You haven't changed a bit!'

I followed his lead. This was turning out to be fun, and

I could see that Cindy could scarcely contain her laughter either.

'Nor have you!' I said, smiling broadly back at him. 'You must meet my friend. Cindy, this is Manuel, we've been friends for ages.'

Manuel kissed Cindy's hand. She leaned over me and whispered, 'Such a touching scene!'

I ignored her and turned back to Manuel, who by now had another man standing next to him.

'I'd like to introduce my friend and colleague, Rodolfo. We had a meeting in Barcelona, and tonight it's his birthday, so we decided to celebrate it here.'

'Pleased to meet you, Rodolfo, and congratulations,' I said, shaking his hand.

'Pleased and congratulations,' Cindy said, imitating me.

Rodolfo was also good-looking, and seemed very friendly. But I preferred Manuel.

'Are you expecting someone?' Manuel asked, before sitting down at our table.

The next problem was going to be who went with whom. As I understood it, Rodolfo was allowed first choice, as this was his night. Manuel was supposed to take the girl his friend did not want.

'No, please, come and join us,' I said, with my best smile.

After a moment's hesitation, Rodolfo sat down next to Cindy. It looked as though he had already made his choice. Manuel sat in the fourth chair, and I felt distinctly relieved.

'Are you still in politics?' I asked him.

'Yes, I have to earn a living.'

It really seemed that both of us had learned our lines perfectly. He leaned closer and whispered to me, 'Your friend knows Rodolfo isn't to suspect a thing, doesn't she?'

'Yes. Don't worry.'

'Fine. And by the way, you look great!' he added, much to my surprise.

'So do you. And I'm glad your friend chose Cindy.'

'So am I. I was scared he wouldn't!' he said, still staring me in the face.

I said nothing. I was rather intimidated by him.

'You're incredible. It's as though we really have been friends all our lives.'

I liked this politician. I wanted to take him to bed with me.

After we had chatted a while with our respective opposite numbers, I remembered I had to ring Susana. I said I needed to go to the bathroom, and got up from the table.

When I rang, it was Angelika who replied. I could tell she was fuming at the end of the line, but I calmed her down. I also replaced the piece of sponge properly. It was still killing me! What a great idea Cristina had! This was the first and last time I was going to put crap like that inside me.

By the time I got back to our table, Rodolfo was feeling very sick. He was about to throw up because of all he had been drinking. Manuel was really sorry, but said he felt he had to take him back to their hotel. I tried to persuade him we could meet up later in his room, but he would have none of it. He did not want to risk it, he said, with his friend in such a state.

Cindy and I were left there like two idiots, not knowing what to say, and feeling frustrated because each of us had liked our client. The Kuwaitis at the next table tried to chat us up again, but I managed to convince Cindy not to have anything to do with them, and soon afterwards we clambered into a taxi to take us back to the apartment.

The Marquis De Sade Waltz

5th September 1999

Four in the afternoon.

The building was opposite the Barceloneta beach, in a part of the city which was far from salubrious.

I agreed to go, among other reasons, because this was the first time Susana had called me during the day, and I felt privileged. I wanted to show her she could always count on me. She had given me precise information about the very special client I was going to see, and as I went up to the third floor I felt well in control, dressed in jeans and a white blouse.

'Don't wear anything sophisticated,' Susana had recommended, 'just jeans and no make-up. He wants a schoolgirl, and you're not exactly fifteen.'

That last gratuitous comment had infuriated me for a while, but gradually the idea of acting out this scene of an adolescent girl had started to excite me. At last, something different! I was beginning to be really fed up with men who just wanted a conventional fuck. After the failure with the two politicians I wanted something that broke the routine, and this sounded interesting.

When I entered the building, I found there was no lift. It was a very old, rundown place, and the ground floor was obviously where all the local youngsters met on a Saturday night: the walls were full of graffiti, and under the stairwell it was black and scorched where someone had tried to set light to it. There were Coke cans littering the floor, and as I went by a few kids started playing football with them, kicking them at me and laughing.

The client lived right at the top. I plucked up my courage and started climbing the stairs two at a time until I reached the fifth floor. I felt nervous, wondering what kind of a guy could possibly live in such a dump.

I had almost got to his door when my mobile rang.

'Hello?'

I had to shout because the kids playing downstairs were making such a racket it could be heard all the way up here.

'Aren't you there yet?' Susana asked me impatiently. 'You've been half an hour in the taxi. What are you up to? The client is waiting for you!'

'I was just about to call you. I've almost reached the front door,' I replied breathlessly. I realized all of a sudden that someone was watching me from the landing.

A swarthy, heavy guy was glaring at me from the door I was walking towards, mobile in hand.

'I have to go now,' I told Susana when I saw him gesticulating at me to switch off my phone at once. He looked furious.

I put my phone away.

He ushered me in quickly without a word. Before shutting the door he glanced up and down the corridor to see if anyone had witnessed the scene.

Then, still without saying anything, he pushed me towards the living room. When we had reached it, he suddenly let rip.

'Not exactly the soul of discretion, are you?'

Until then I had almost thought he must be mute. But his voice was so gruff I began to feel even more nervous.

'I'm sorry! You're right, I should have switched it off.'

'I told your boss: no mobiles! I don't want my neighbours to know I pay for a whore!'

I hated the word, yet he didn't look like someone I wanted to get into an argument with.

'How old are you?'

'Twenty-two.'

'I asked for a younger girl.'

He lit a cigarette. I said nothing. I'd already lied by taking eight years off my age. The atmosphere in the room made me even uneasier. It smelt of ancient furniture and dust, and I tried desperately to relax.

'You're so lucky to have a flat with a sea view!' I said, moving towards his balcony.

'You're joking! Can't you see it's a shit-hole?'

He was right there. It was an old flat full of old furniture, with one crumbling sofa. The floor was covered in cheap tiles scored with black marks where the pieces of furniture had been moved over the years. The walls were covered in a faded yellow paper that was torn in several places, revealing the white plaster underneath. It was obvious that none of the tenants had ever looked after the place.

'Yes, but you've got the sea,' I insisted.

'I couldn't give a fuck about the sea! This is a shit-hole!'

Of course, he was bound to contradict anything I said. He slumped onto the sofa which was covered in an old check blanket, whose only functions as far as I could tell were to keep the settee together, and to produce filthy balls of fluff. This was going to be hard work. The guy was obviously a bitter loner and I was obviously not what he wanted.

'Come over here so I can get a better look at you.'

By now he was flat on his back on the sofa. I went over to him, and he got me to twirl round so he could examine me front and back. Then he took his trousers down and told me to do the same. He stood up again, his underpants covered in fluff, and went over to the stereo. He put on a CD.

'Do you dance?' he asked.

'Yes,' I said, hoping a bit of music might calm him down.

Five minutes later he had had enough of music and dancing. He ordered, 'Now, get down on all fours.'

He got the money out of his trouser pocket and threw it on the floor in front of me.

I stared at him for a minute, trying to understand what he wanted, then did as he had asked.

As I knelt down, he jumped on my back like a rider on a horse. By now I was convinced I was faced with a raving lunatic, whose only wish was to humiliate me. That was all I needed! He started riding me, then grabbed hold of my hair like a caveman. He was so heavy, my coccyx was grating against my lower back.

'What are you doing?' I shouted, trying to get up.

'Don't you like it?'

'What do you mean? You're hurting me.'

'I'm paying, so I can do what I want!'

'Oh no,' I said, red-faced, 'that's where you're wrong. I don't work for a sadomaso agency. If you want to humiliate a girl, there are people who specialize in that! But I'm not one of them.'

I could feel a sense of fear gripping my body, because I had no idea how this madman might react.

'Yes, you're right, I wanted to humiliate someone, and I thought any whore would do. But I can see you don't want to collaborate,' he said scornfully.

My heart was pounding uncontrollably.

'I'm sorry, but I'm not any whore, as you call them. If you want, I'll leave. You'll only have to pay the taxi.' As I said it, I was hoping against hope he would agree.

The atmosphere was unbearable.

'No, no, don't do that! Call your agency and tell them you're staying the hour.'

By now I didn't understand a thing.

'No violence then, all right?'

'Don't worry,' he said, looking daggers at me. 'No violence.'

Despite myself, I called Susana. I really didn't want to stay with this weirdo, and hoped she would be able to hear the fear in my voice and tell me to come back at once, without running any more risks. But she said nothing.

'Now let's go to the bedroom,' he said as soon as I finished. I didn't like this new tone of voice either.

He showed me into a small, filthy bedroom. In it was

a single bed with a stained sheet on it. He took my undies off, and literally threw me onto the bed.

Then he disappeared into the bathroom. I took advantage of being alone to take a good look round me, trying to understand what kind of person I was having to do this with. On a bookshelf I saw all kinds of books with scary titles, and the complete works of the Marquis de Sade in Spanish. Next to them were fetish objects, and on the wall hung a very long whip and a leather mask. God, I'm in Hannibal Lecter's house, I told myself.

He came out of the bathroom wearing only a tiny thong, and started pacing up and down like an exhibitionist.

'Just look and say nothing,' he said, with his wild, staring eyes on me.

The thong was squashing his genitals so much he soon had to tear it off. He put a condom on and leapt on me, searching for my vagina with clumsy fingers. Thank god pharmaceutical laboratories have invented glycerine!

He penetrated me roughly, howling obscenities. I had only one thing in mind: to finish as quickly as possible and get out of there. His revolting body weighed like a hundred-ton boulder on top of me, and every time he thrust forward, a wild animal smell filled my nostrils. As he came, his whole quivering mass started trembling and shaking uncontrollably. It was unbearable. When everything was finally over, I scooped up my clothes without a word to him, and ran to the door, putting them on as I went. I ran down the stairs and outside, where the youngsters from before were surprisingly quiet. I sprinted down the street like an Olympic athlete. I wanted to get as far away as possible from that freak and leave behind all the foul language he had slobbered all over me. I was hoping that as I ran, the wind would wipe me clean of his words. When I couldn't breathe any more, I came to a halt and allowed all the tears I had been holding back, all my accumulated rage, to come tumbling out of me.

In The Eye Of The Camera

6th September 1999

Six in the morning.

'Susana told me all about it,' Cristina said, with little trace of compassion in her voice, when she arrived at my flat. 'It takes all sorts, and you'll just have to get used to it, because you're sure to meet more of them.'

'He nearly injured me,' I pointed out.

My voice was hoarse because I had barely slept, and because I was in a bad mood. The last thing I felt like was posing for a camera, but I knew my job depended on it.

A car was waiting for us out in the street. Ignacio the photographer was the driver, and beside him sat his assistant, who was going to help keep my make-up fresh.

'I also forget to tell you how important it is for you to call Susana as soon as you get to the client's place. If you don't, we'll think you arrived sooner and have got him to pay you extra. It's happened before with other girls, and now Susana is suspicious of everyone. The same when you leave. We need to know the exact time: if the client wants you to stay longer, you have to call Susana and tell her.'

'I was going to call her, but she got in first. The client lived a long way away, and with all the traffic I was late arriving. But I didn't spend any longer with him, Cristina!'

'Susana is convinced you did.'

When I protested again, Cristina wanted to close the argument.

'It doesn't matter this time,' she said. 'But don't let it happen again!'

I glanced at her, horrified, but said nothing. It seemed like this was going to be a difficult morning.

After that, we hardly spoke on the drive. All of us were very tired. I was the worst, although I was beginning to get used to being woken at any hour. I was angry with Susana as well. I couldn't understand how she could think and say things like that about me. Whatever my faults, I'm not a cheat.

Before we began the photo session, we stopped at a village bar for some breakfast.

'Cristina tells me you're getting on well in the agency,' Ignacio said, to break the silence.

'Yes, everything's fine for now.'

'You'll see, with a book of photos you'll get twice the work,' he said, convinced the photobook would be my best investment ever.

'I hope so!'

I drank several cappuccinos, and began to feel better. I was anxious to make a start.

Nothing special happened today, except for the usual row with Isa. She's had something stolen again. This time it was what she claimed was a gold bracelet and the Cartier rings she was given by the old guy she's been living off for the past three months.

I was in the living room when I heard her shouting hysterically, then talking to Sara, the Barbie doll.

'I bet it was that Frenchwoman,' she told her.

I preferred to keep my cool, because if I didn't, I knew I might attack her. And I wouldn't do that, because I suspected that she was just trying to get me thrown out of the agency.

Isa and Sara stormed into the kitchen to see Susana. I tried to make out what they were saying, but from where I was sitting their words were unintelligible. A few moments later Susana came out of her headquarters, cigarette in hand.

'Can I speak to you for a moment, sweetheart?' she said, in a non-committal sort of voice.

I knew very well what she wanted to talk about, so I nodded.

'Look, I don't know what's going on with you! The other day, Isa's Versace jacket disappears. Then I send you out to a client and you take forever to get there. Now Isa claims someone's stolen her gold bracelet and rings. I'm sorry, but that's a lot of coincidences since you arrived.'

'What are you implying?' I said, sick of being accused without proof.

'No, nothing. But it all seems very strange to me, sweetheart.'

'Are you insinuating it was me who stole Isa's jacket and her jewellery?' I was furious.

'No, I'm not saying it was you, just that it's very strange.'

'Don't you think it's because I'm new here, and Isa can't stand the sight of me? Can't you see she's trying to set everyone against me? She can't stand me, Susana, and I'm beginning to think you can't either.'

'What's that, sweetheart? No, you're wrong there. I'm just doing my job. Whenever there are problems between girls, I have to sort them out. I don't want it to be like last time, when Isa called Manolo at home. If that happens, I'm the one with problems.'

As if on cue, the front door opened and Manolo came in, wearing the same pair of shorts with loafers. This time, his bumbag looked empty.

'Don't say anything to him,' Susana warned me. 'I'll talk to him.'

'What's going on here?' he complained. 'I don't want any secret meetings.'

'Nothing's going on, Manolo. We're only talking.'

Susana's voice was quavering, and she was lying so unconvincingly anyone could have spotted it. It was obvious she was terrified of Manolo.

'Well if nothing's going on, why don't you get back into the kitchen, idiot!'

This made me feel very sorry for Susana. He was treating her like a dog.

As she ran into the kitchen, Isa and Sara came out.

'What are you two doing in there anyway?' Manolo wanted to know.

'Can I have a word with you, Manolo?' Isa asked him.

She glared at me, and I realized she was going to tell him what had happened. I decided to keep my mouth shut and await the outcome. Isa disappeared into the small bedroom with Manolo. They were in there for quite a while before the two of them reappeared.

'No problem. I'm glad you told me in plenty of time. Of course you can have a fortnight off over Christmas,' Manolo said to Isa, before saying goodbye to us all.

Isa hadn't told him a thing. She simply said she wanted to go and see her family in Ecuador in December. But she had put on this whole show just to frighten me. As Manolo left, she looked at me as if to say, 'Next time, you're for it!'

Plastic Fantastic

15th September 1999

The Barbie doll doesn't speak, doesn't have any opinions, doesn't smile, and doesn't look at anything around her. All she does is see to her hair. For hours on end. David, the Australian client I was with on the first night I met Angelika, came to the brothel. He came because he had been out on the town with some friends and after all the discos had closed he didn't want to go home on his own, so decided to come and offer himself some pleasure.

He had never been with Barbie, because she had never been available when he had called. But tonight she was. So Barbie paraded in front of him, her hair immaculate after all the hours she had spent grooming herself in front of the mirror. He chose her straight away.

'She's fascinating,' he confessed to Angelika. 'I've never seen tits like it!'

Proud of herself, the Barbie doll disappeared with him into the suite.

Ten minutes later she came running out, stark naked, and crying her eyes out. Seeing her like that unexpectedly, our jaws dropped. Curiosity about what happens to any of the girls is what gives spice to our lives in the apartment, so we all wanted to know what had happened to her. Had the client tried to harm her? I sincerely doubted that, because, at least when I was with him, David had shown himself to be kind and considerate. Had he changed his mind, and got suddenly scared of being smothered by those two huge breasts? Did Barbie do a Cuban with him and squash his prick without meaning to, thanks to all that silicone? All these unsolved mysteries . . . the atmosphere was electric.

A few moments after Barbie had appeared, David came rushing out, demanding his money back.

'She's not a woman!' he shouted. 'She's a transvestite!'

He was beside himself.

'What are you talking about, David?' Angelika challenged him. 'She's not a transvestite. She's a real woman, I swear.'

'And I tell you she's a transvestite who's had an operation. And besides, her tits are as hard as rocks! They're disgusting. I bet she's had a sex change.'

'Well yes, she's had operations. But on her breasts, that's all. I swear to you Sara is a woman.'

'She's a transvestite. Give me my money back right now!'

'But . . .'

Angelika tried in vain to convince him. David would not budge, and Sara started to insult him, then burst into tears.

'How dare he say my tits are like rocks? The best

plastic surgeon in Spain operated on me. And it cost me a fortune!'

That was the first and only time I heard Sara's voice.

20th September 1999

I'm beginning to feel more and more at ease in the brothel. All the girls apart from Isa have accepted me. She is as foul to me as she is to everyone else. And apart from my good relations with the other girls, I am starting to have regular clients. I'm happy, and all the nervousness of the first days has disappeared.

I feel good about my body, and above all about my mind. The truth is, the work is no harder than any other job. After the first stormy days, I am getting used to a routine which allows me to enjoy what I do and to live my liberated sexuality as best I can.

After the episode with the Barbie doll, David only wants to be with me. Well, that's what he says. I know he calls other agencies and sees other girls. He enjoys sex, and I know the rules of the game. Twice a week with me is not enough for him. And even though he's not my kind of guy, I get a lot of pleasure from doing it with him.

I have also got another regular. At first he was meant to see another girl, but she wasn't available. His name is Pedro.

21st September 1999

I was with an American in the Princesa Sofia Hotel when Angelika called to say that as soon as I had finished I was to take a taxi to a hotel on the outskirts of Barcelona.

She had already sent Gina, a blonde girl who occasionally works in the agency to help pay for a new Mercedes she bought, but when she arrived, she discovered the client was . . . her boss! She could hardly believe it! Gina ran off, got into her brand new Mercedes, and drove at a hundred and eighty kilometres an hour back to the apartment in a state of shock. Fortunately there was only a dim light in the corridor, so her boss had not recognized her when he opened the door, and he had no idea what had happened. But the poor man was left frustrated, and was waiting impatiently for a replacement.

When I first met Pedro, he struck me as a nervous, almost neurotic guy, with thinning hair. I tried to be sympathetic, and he took an immediate liking to me. They say opposite poles attract, but that was only true in his case. Pedro lives in a hotel five days a week, near the company he runs. At the weekend he goes home and plays the role of the good father and husband.

That night when we went to bed he was very insistent I give him a blow job without protection. He said he hadn't been near his wife in four years. When I refused to do anything unprotected, he started to bawl like a baby and then, when he got inside me, he came in five minutes. I felt no pleasure at all. He was very sweet, but a disastrous lover. I consoled myself with the thought that at least I'd had a profitable day.

23rd September 1999

Pedro is becoming obsessed with me. He called to find out if I was free, then came early to see if I could spend the whole night with him. First he paid for a few hours and we went to the suite. He told me he wasn't really that interested in sex. What he wanted above all from me was a kind of psychologist or counsellor. And if it was someone with their legs open, better still!

I felt a special affection for him. Of course I preferred to be with him because he treated me well, rather than with some degenerate who could ask me to do revolting tricks. Pedro said he thought he was doing it for my good, because that way I didn't have to go with other men. Afterwards, he decided to take me out to dance, warning me in advance that he was a poor drinker. I on the contrary can drink whatever's thrown at me. I think it's because I am just being reborn, and have an inner strength that helps me overcome anything. Tonight I decided to use that to my advantage. He took me for a drink in a bar in the city centre, and all of a sudden declared that he was thinking of proposing to me. He even wanted to give me a white-gold ring. I turned him down flat.

'I don't want you to propose to me. I don't want to marry anybody. Besides, at the moment I'm not capable of loving anyone. I want to make some money, pay my debts, and move on!'

'I'll do everything I can to make you love me, I promise.'

'Don't you get it, I don't want to fall in love! And anyway, you're not my kind of guy at all. I'm sorry.'

The more I rejected him, the more eager he became. It was a challenge to him, apparently the first he had ever had to face. My rejection only made him cling to me all the more, because, as he said helplessly, what he most wanted was an authoritarian woman at his side. I think that deep down he was delighted with the idea that he could be a good Samaritan and save a desperate girl from her misery. That flattered his vanity and gave some point to his boring existence. But I was physically revolted by Pedro, and I wanted to make sure we did not have any further sexual contact. His prick is like a thin strand of spaghetti whose only real function is to hang down limply between his legs. Nothing more.

We began to dance, and just seeing him jigging around on the dance floor made me feel sorry for him again. He was stiffer than a block of wood. I kept asking for more whisky, and then pouring it into his glass. He didn't seem to notice. I had decided not to give him my body: I was already doing more than enough by putting up with all his moaning. Then suddenly he announced, 'I'm going to get a divorce.'

'Are things so bad at home?' I asked.

I couldn't believe he was being serious. Apart from anything else, by now he was completely drunk.

'I feel such a fool there. Ever since I met you, I realize how much I have been duping myself all these years. I can't bear my wife any more, and my marriage is a complete farce.'

'Well, if that's the way it is, be brave and change your life. But do it for yourself, not for me. Don't ask me to help you any more than I am doing. I don't want to be your lover and have no other ties.'

'I don't want you to be my lover, I want you to marry me!'

'You're only fooling yourself again, Pedro. You've fallen in love with someone you met in a very special context. You know you're free to come and go as you please. You pay, and that's all there is to it. But in real life it would be different, you'd soon get fed up with me.'

'What are you saying? You can't imagine how much I love you! I love you more than my own son!'

This sounded so extreme and worrying that I decided to make sure he had some more whisky. I can't bear that kind of talk, and couldn't imagine what kind of love he might have for his son. He really wasn't in his right mind. I didn't want to hear another word on the subject.

'I don't know what a woman like you is doing in a place like that. You shouldn't be there. Why do you do it, when you've got a university degree and everything?'

'I do it because people like you exist!' I retorted angrily.

What's wrong? Was it so wrong for someone with a degree, someone who had held down an executive position, to work as a prostitute? Did it make me a criminal or a bad person or something? Pedro was staring at me, but apparently didn't understand a thing.

A short while later he began to feel very ill, and I had to drag him out of the nightclub while everyone looked on in surprise. I almost had to carry him out. Pedro does not weigh much more than me, but we must have looked very comical.

When we were out in the street, I faced another huge problem: how to persuade a taxi-driver to take us back to Pedro's hotel. What made it so difficult was the fact that they took one look at him and were afraid he would throw up all over their cab. Finally a good-hearted plump old man agreed to take us, probably because he had not realized how bad Pedro was, since I had left him slumped on a bench while I found someone. En route, though, we had to suddenly pull over to the hard shoulder when my companion threatened to bring up everything he had drunk that night all over the seat. Fortunately he didn't do so, but the driver started shouting insults at me, insisting I had tried to trick him. I was so embarrassed I could do nothing but excuse myself.

When we reached the hotel, I steeled myself to make Pedro vomit at all costs. If I didn't, I was going to have to spend the night awake, keeping an eye on him. By now he was threatening to throw himself out of the window because he was in love with a woman who didn't love him. This melodramatic attitude was the last straw, so I took hold of him from behind in the bathroom, pushed him towards the toilet with my arms round his stomach, and squeezed as hard as I could until he started to bring everything up. He was sick as a dog, then staggered off to bed. Eventually I managed to get to sleep too.

The next morning Pedro woke up with a hangover to end all hangovers. He was chain-smoking cigarettes until I woke up. I had succeeded in escaping from the sexual relation I found so repugnant, and I felt proud of the little game I had played. I went back to the agency happy and fresh as a daisy.

'You like that client a lot, don't you?' Susana asked me as I came in.

It wasn't so much a question as an affirmation. There was no way I was going to tell her I was so happy because I had earned my money for nothing. I knew by now that she was quite capable of telling Manolo and Cristina, and that would only cause problems.

Susana had turned out to be not only nosey, but an informer.

'I bet you have a great time in bed with him.'

In response I smiled sweetly, took my money, and went home.

My Turn To Pay . . .

25th September 1999

When Susana called I was in the gym. Fortunately as ever I had my mobile with me. The ringing tone echoed round the walls of the huge room I go to several times a week. I had to answer in a whisper so as not to draw attention to myself: the other members already looked annoyed that their exercise had been interrupted by the noise.

'You have to come at once. There are no girls here, and the client has chosen you from your photo.'

'Susana, I'm in the gym. I'll get ready, but it's going to take time.'

'Hurry up then!'

I always take a change of clothes with me in case something like this happens, and today I was glad I had thought ahead, because it meant I didn't have to go home first. I got dressed in the changing room, found a taxi, and went straight to the agency.

It had rained a little in the morning and it was a grey

day, so I wasn't feeling too bright, but work is work.

Susana was waiting impatiently for me. She always gets nervous: she takes her work so seriously she could never accept that a client had slipped through her fingers because a girl had taken too long to get to the agency. So she lives on her nerves, and as a result suffers badly from psoriasis. She's also permanently frightened they're going to throw her out, and so she never helps us feel relaxed. This attitude of hers was partly responsible for my feeling much closer to Angelika, who is capable of being much more flexible than her.

'Come on, go in and meet him before he disappears . . .'

'All right, Susana. I was at the other end of Barcelona; I couldn't get here any faster.'

I tidied my hair in the mirror, then went into the living room. The client was watching TV, with a glass of rum and Coke in his hand. He gave the impression of having already drunk several of the same. When he saw me, he smiled, but said nothing, so I had to start the conversation. It turned out he was an aeronautical engineer, married with a family (they all are), but he felt very lonely. He was not in the least good-looking, in fact he was positively repulsive in appearance, and yet there was something charismatic about him.

When I sat down next to him, I was amazed at the effect I produced: he started literally to tremble. He confessed he felt very scared, which I found endearing, so I did my best to help him relax, and we went into the suite. He took off his clothes shyly, then got into bed and covered himself completely so that I wouldn't see him naked. Not exactly promising! I thought this was bound to be another sexual disaster, but . . . in fact it was fantastic! I came without even having to fake it. I loved the way he caressed my whole body. He was such an expert in female anatomy I could hardly believe this was the same gauche man I had met a few minutes earlier in the living room.

When it was over and he had gone off for a shower, I took my purse out of my bag, and offered him fifty thousand pesetas.

'What's that for?' he asked, rubbing his body briskly with the towel.

'I'm giving you back what you paid Susana to be with me,' I said in a whisper, to make sure the microphones did not pick up my voice.

'What . . . ?

'You heard me . . . please, take it!'

'But why?'

'To thank you for what you gave me. Today, it's my turn to pay. But don't expect the same every time . . . and don't say a word to Susana,' I said, smiling at him.

I had to insist to get him to take the money, but he finally accepted it, saying, 'I understand women less and less.'

As he was leaving, I murmured to him, 'There's nothing to understand.'

In reality I was telling myself that, because he wasn't even my type.

State of Siege

This morning, Manolo and Angelika had a big row. I was asleep in the small bedroom until the lorry driver's shouts woke me up. I could also make out Angelika's voice raised in anger, so I went to see what was going on. I knew I was in a madhouse, where anything could happen.

None of the other girls had batted an eyelid. When 'the boss' gets angry, it's out of their league, they say. Or 'mind your own business', as Mae put it to me one day. But this time I couldn't help myself: it sounded as though Manolo was about to hit Angelika, and I felt I had to do something.

In the kitchen, Manolo was taking Angelika to task. Amongst other things, he claimed that the previous night she had not been doing her job, but had gone to sleep. The proof, he said, was that when he had called at four in the morning, I was the one who had answered.

'You forgot that we record everything, idiot!' Manolo

was bellowing. 'We've got Val's voice on tape. Why was she answering instead of you? You're meant to be in charge, aren't you?'

I could see Angelika was getting very upset, so I decided to intervene.

'She was in the bathroom,' I explained, trying to provide her with an alibi.

'Do you want to end up on the street as well?' Manolo said, shouting even louder. 'Why are you trying to defend her by lying? We know she was asleep. You yourself told Isa so. We recorded that too.'

I thought back to the previous night, and realized it was true. I'd really put my foot in it this time. Angelika and I exchanged looks, then she gathered her things and said she hadn't the slightest intention of staying a moment longer in a madhouse like this, where everything she did was spied on even more than in the Big Brother house.

'That's right! Get your things: you know where the door is!' Manolo shouted after her.

Angelika slammed the door so hard on her way out, the whole neighbourhood must have heard it.

'Don't worry,' Manolo reassured me, 'there'll be a new person here tonight. And this time she'll be a real professional!'

I found it hard to conceal my dismay, because Angelika was the only person I could talk freely to in the brothel. I also felt it was partly my fault she had been thrown out. All I had was her phone number, and I told myself I would call soon to keep in touch.

I felt upset all day at the way Angelika had been treated, then in the evening I went back to the agency to work. I was met by a new manager, a girl called Dolores, who looked as much of a call girl as the rest of us. She was on the thin side, with a good figure, long jet-black hair and huge honey-coloured eyes. A real doll. We said hello briefly, and I could tell she was making a great effort to be friendly. That seemed normal enough. Anybody would be apprehensive at meeting so many girls for the first time, and she felt she had to win us all over.

But when I went into the living room to leave my things, I had a big surprise. The girls were sitting there in silence, and they all looked very worried. This was the first time I felt they were all united.

They were all smoking cigarettes, and had obviously been doing so for some time, because all the ashtrays were full of butts. I could tell something was wrong and that they were very nervous. Cindy was the first to speak.

'Sit down and shut the door.'

I did as she said. Something was not right.

'What's the matter with you all? Why are you sitting here like this?' I asked, beginning to be worried myself.

'What's the matter?' Isa echoed.

'Can't you see?' Mae chimed in.

'It's a disaster!' said Estefania.

'I can kiss my Mercedes goodbye!' Gina reflected out loud, staring into space.

As usual, the only one who said nothing was Barbie doll. I was sure she was planning her next session of plastic surgery.

'We're finished!' Cindy exclaimed.

I still didn't understand what they were talking about.

277

What could have happened to have affected them like this? What could have made them all be in agreement for once? It was as though all their disputes had vanished by magic.

'Why are we finished?' I wanted to know.

I couldn't stand to be kept in the dark any longer.

'That woman . . .' Isa began.

'She's sure to steal all our clients!' Mae finished for her.

'What do you mean? She's the new night manager. Angelika was turfed out this morning, and Manolo told me they were going to take on a real professional,' I explained, trying to calm them all down. 'Why would she steal our clients?'

'Because she's so pretty,' Estefania said. 'And as soon as she realizes that they are only paying her a pittance compared to what we earn, she'll start stealing our clients. You'll see! It's already happened here a long time ago.'

'But that would be awful!'

'They should never employ such an attractive manager. It's always risky. I don't understand why Manolo did it!' said Gina.

The Barbie doll nodded, making sure her hair didn't fly off at the same time.

'Well, if you all say so . . . what shall we do?'

'We have to stick together,' said Cindy, 'and we're counting on you!'

'Yes, we have to keep an eye on her and listen to everything she says to the clients. If there's the slightest doubt, we tell Manolo,' Isa said forcefully.

'All right, you can count on me, but I really don't think things will go that far.'

'You'll see,' Gina predicted. 'But for now, back to work as normal.'

Losing Angelika like that had brought us all together. We decided to 'mount guard'. When not all of us were in the agency, those who were working had to keep a close eye on Dolores. That first night, she did her job exactly as she was supposed to: she was pleasant with us all, and we had nothing to reproach her with. Not a thing! I was beginning to think we could relax our state of high-security alert.

4th October 1999

Today there were a lot of calls from foreigners who did not speak a word of Spanish. And the problems with Dolores started. As I'm the only girl who speaks other languages, Dolores came in several times during the night to ask me to deal with them. I thought this was a bit much, but I agreed, as we all knew that sooner or later Manolo was going to find out what was going on, and this would be the perfect excuse to get rid of her. The agency telephone is tapped and at some point either he or Cristina would hear me speaking. Dolores had told them she spoke perfect English and French, so they would soon realize she had been lying to them.

The very next morning Manolo turned up at the brothel to talk to Dolores, or rather, to shout at her. He told her in no uncertain terms that he did not care how she did it, but that she was in charge and was the person who was supposed to take the calls, not us.

After this, Dolores began to sense that she was bound to lose her job sooner or later, and began to try to seduce all the clients. This was after a conversation I had with her.

'Val, how much do you earn in a week?'

'That depends, Dolores. It varies from week to week.'

'Yes, but let's say on average . . .'

'Between six and seven hundred thousand pesetas.'

I was deliberately exaggerating a bit.

'How much? That's crazy! And I'm only getting two hundred thousand a month! That's not right!'

'No, but I have to open my legs to get it, and you don't. So it seems fair enough to me.'

She thought about it, and I could see she was already considering how she could keep a few clients for herself and earn as much as possible before she lost her job. So the girls had been right.

6th October 1999

Today we caught Dolores giving her phone number to a client who visits us every week. We called Manolo, and although Dolores denied everything, by that afternoon she was out on her ear.

'Get your things, and out into the fucking street with you!' Manolo shouted at her.

Revolving Doors

7th October 1999

After the fiasco with Dolores, the other girls no longer look at me as if I were the one who stole Isa's clothes. And strangely enough, there have been no more robberies in the brothel.

The arrival today of Sofia was like a whiff of oxygen in a cardboard box full of tiny holes. She is around fifty, and looks like a leftover hippy in her long multicoloured skirts, her huge hooped earrings and a velvet hat. Right from the start, we all felt we would get on very well with this new night manager. She's educated, gentle and there's something about her that reminds me of my paternal grandmother. Her real passion is caring for animals; she adores them and is forever rescuing whatever four-legged creature she finds abandoned on the street.

I have always believed that animal lovers must be kind-hearted and incapable of doing others harm. In Sofia's case I'm right. She's a sweet person, and extraordinarily generous.

Sofia has a little dog which she named Jordi to emphasize its Catalan roots, although these are non-existent. He's a mongrel she found in a street in Paris, where she spent long periods with a lover, ten years earlier. Now, Jordi means everything to her: she's even asked Manolo if she can bring him to the apartment sometimes, because she says that if she leaves him on his own, he gets depressed. Our lorry driver said yes, provided the dog did not bark in the middle of the night. I'm beginning to suspect that even Manolo has a heart.

I spent the whole night with Pedro, and when I returned in the morning, I offered to take Jordi out for a walk. As she was handing me the money I'd earned for the night and passing over Jordi, Sofia gave me a piece of advice.

'Don't be stupid. As soon as you've finished paying off your debts, start saving. Don't do like the other girls, and spend it all on more clothes. Save as much as you can! And above all, don't fall in love!'

But when love comes to call and it's true love, it's hard to resist. That's what happened to me in this most unlikely of places, and with the most unexpected person. It was the tenth of October 1999.

I Meet Giovanni

10th October 1999

A little more than a month has gone by, and having sex with strangers no longer holds any kind of interest for me. It's becoming nothing more than gymnastics. In these few weeks I've earned almost two million pesetas, and if this continues, I'll be able to pay back my debts much more quickly than I had ever thought. If all goes well, I'll have settled everything within five months. I intend to carry on working in the brothel for a little longer than that, to make sure I am back on my feet financially, and then change my life again.

This afternoon I was at home doing housework when Susana called.

'Come quickly, I've got two Italian clients waiting for you. You have to hurry, because they've got a plane to catch. Is that all right, sweetheart?'

'That's fine. I'll be there, but you know I can't fly. I'll get there as soon as I can. Tell them to wait.'

I got ready as quickly as I could. I only had to put on

some make-up, then ran out into the street to catch a taxi. It must have been fate . . . not a single one free. More than half an hour had gone by since Susana first phoned, when my mobile rang again.

'What are you doing, sweetheart? If you don't hurry up, I'll have to call another girl.'

'I know, Susana. I'm trying to take a taxi, but it's rush hour with everyone leaving work, and I can't find one free. Please tell the clients I'm on my way, but there's a lot of traffic. Please, Susana!'

On another day I would have got angry with her, but today something told me it was best to stay calm. I finally reached the agency an hour later, with my eyeliner all smudged from sweating in the taxi. Susana was furious, and the two Italians were on the point of leaving.

I went into the living room straight away. They were both very elegant, as only Italian men know how to be. One, called Alessandro, was short, fat and bald. The other was tall and thin, with a twinkle in his eye that made me warm to him immediately. Giovanni was not good-looking, but his face was calm and gentle. Unfortunately, as ever, it was not up to me to choose. I walked over to the small bedroom, and found Estefania and Mae sitting there. Both of them had already been out to show themselves, but only Estefania had been chosen: by Alessandro. I felt extremely relieved that I was going with the one I had liked best.

Mae was left empty-handed, sitting on the bed smoking a cigarette. She didn't seem to hold it against me too much, because by now we had established a sort of code of honour between us: 'It was me the client chose, so back off!'

When Giovanni and I went into the suite, he took a quick shower. I undressed, and when he came out of the bathroom he took me in this arms. I was surprised, because clients never normally do that: they prefer to get straight into bed. We embraced each other for a few moments, then he looked at me tenderly and we kissed. We both wanted to go on kissing; there was a kind of energy between the two of us that drew us together like magnets.

We were surprised at the strength of this feeling, and starting talking, about Italy and why he had come to Spain. While we were doing so, we could hear the groans of pleasure from the next room, where both Estefania and Alessandro seemed to be enjoying themselves. Our own sexual activity never reached such heights. In the end, I masturbated Giovanni because he was too tired to attempt anything else. I was more than satisfied with the kiss he had given me. What had happened between us was something special. I had the feeling I had known him all my life: his smell, his smile, his hands. When he left he said he would be back in two days, and hoped to see me again. He also asked what my real name was.

'The one I told you. Val is my real name, I promise you.'

'Dai! Non é vero. So che it tuo nome é differente.' (Come on, that's not true. I know your real name is different.)

'No, no, believe me. I don't use a different name for work, if that's what you mean.'

He left the apartment laughing, promising that the next time I would tell him my real name and give him my phone number. I don't know anything about him, and I have no idea whether I will see him again. Men promise so many things they never do. And yet deep down inside, something told me I would run into him again.

The Glass Man

11th October 1999

Meeting Giovanni made me think a lot about the path I have taken until now. I think fate is always playing with people, and that there are many different paths. I chose one, and, my lesson learnt, I ended up meeting Giovanni in a brothel. If I had never decided to become a prostitute, I would never have met him. We seem to have so little in common that the chances of our meeting were extremely remote . . . Deep down, all I am looking for is love. Blind dates, one-night stands, the brothel, all are simply means to try to find what I've always been searching for. Today I felt very pleased at my discovery, and wanted to show the whole world.

So with this wonderful feeling in my body, I went to work as usual, determined to spread a little happiness all around me. Little did I know that my 'victim' that night was perhaps the person most in need of it that I had yet to meet.

Sofia woke me at two in the morning, Jordi in her

arms. I had a client. A new young man had called and asked for a European girl, someone who was particularly affectionate.

'You'll understand why when you get here,' the client had explained to Sofia.

Isa and I were the only girls working that night, and Sofia knew she could not send her. Instead, she sent me to the client's flat, which was in the upper part of the city, in a very nice building that had twenty-four-hour security.

When the client opened the door, I was unable to hide the surprise and fear on my face, even though I tried to stay as normal as possible. Iñigo greeted me with a smile, sitting comfortably in his wheelchair. He showed me straight into his living room, 'because there'd be no point taking you into the bedroom', as he said with a laugh. It was a large modern apartment, but there was a stale smell I found hard to take. All the doors were specially adapted to let a wheelchair through, and I began to feel very sorry for the boy, who could not have been more than twenty-six.

'I'm almost completely disabled,' he said, in the most natural way in the world.

When he said that, I almost collapsed into a corner of the sofa, then asked him if he minded me smoking.

'I smoke as well,' he said. 'Could you light me one, and put it in my mouth?'

I immediately did as he asked, anxious to please him. He took several puffs on the cigarette, then appealed to me with his eyes to remove it. That was enough for him.

'Thanks!' he said. 'And now, do you think you could

lift me and put me down on the sofa? I could do it, but it takes such an effort.'

I felt a great deal of respect for him, which made me hesitate for a few moments before I picked him up: I was afraid he might fall and shatter like a glass figurine.

'Don't be afraid,' he said. 'Don't worry, I can't feel a thing. The only places where I have any sensation are in my neck and a little in my hands.'

He seemed to have read my mind.

When I had settled him on the sofa, he asked me to take his clothes off. He was skinny; all his limbs had atrophied and his legs were no thicker than my arms. I felt very uncomfortable. To my astonishment, his small – tiny – prick was erect.

'It's like that all the time since my accident. It's not that I'm aroused,' he explained, 'I don't feel a thing down there.'

He burst out laughing again. I felt really stupid, and inwardly cursed myself for ever having wished myself dead. What right did I have to feel so miserable when real suffering was right there in front of my eyes, in the shape of this boy, who bore it with such vitality and good humour?

Obviously, nothing happened between us. I spent the hour giving him kisses all over his neck, and he thanked me from time to time with little moans.

I went back to the agency determined never to complain again. I resolved not to say a word about Iñigo to any of the other girls or the managers. Fate had sent me this episode to make me react, to live the present and seize whatever opportunity arises, without thinking twice about it.

What's He Like? Where Did He Fall In Love With You?

12th October 1999

Giovanni called again. Yes, he's called again! He did as he said he would. And he said he would be waiting for me, with Alessandro, at four o'clock in the agency. Susana told me this morning, and I was jumping up and down I was so happy.

'What's up, sweetheart? You sound as if you'd heard wedding bells!'

Obviously, I had to control myself to some extent with her, otherwise she might have got suspicious. I had no intention of giving Giovanni my phone number on his second visit. First, because I wanted to get to know him a bit better. And second, because I didn't want to risk problems at the brothel. They keep a close watch on me, and I'm afraid of the owners.

This time, Alessandro decided to spend an hour with Mae. He obviously liked her second time around. When I went into the living room I saw Giovanni on his own, waiting for me. I was late again. But his smile when I came into the room told me his desire to see me was stronger than his impatience.

This time we had to use the small bedroom, as Alessandro had taken the suite. We weren't as comfortable as we might have been, but we didn't care. We made love more passionately than I could have believed possible in a place like this. We indulged in all kinds of games, and when his time was up, Susana had to knock on the door to remind us the session was over.

'Give me your phone number,' Giovanni said all of a sudden.

'No, I'm sorry, I can't,' I replied, without explanation.

'Why not? Don't you want to see me again? You could travel with me sometimes. I'd pay you the same, if that's what's worrying you.'

'Of course I want to see you again. But not outside the apartment.'

I pointed up at the ceiling, to try to get him to understand our conversation was being recorded.

'What's wrong?'

He didn't seem to get it, and took hold of my hands as though begging me to tell him what was going on.

I searched in my bag for a biro and a piece of paper, and wrote on it: 'They've put microphones in the room.'

He took the pen from me and wrote: 'Give me your phone number, *per piacere*.'

I didn't give it him. I was dying to, but for some reason I chose not to. Giovanni was sad when he left, but promised he'd be back on 25th November to spend a whole night with me, outside the apartment. That's a long way off, and I didn't know how I was going to be able to bear his absence. This second meeting with

Giovanni made a great impression on me, and I'm sure it's going to affect my work in the brothel. I'm completely torn, because I think he could be the great love of my life, but I don't know what he feels. He liked me a lot, but probably nothing more than that. I could hardly imagine he had fallen head over heels in love with me.

Accident At Work

22nd October 1999

I'm still on cloud nine, ten days after my meeting with Giovanni. I have no way of getting in touch with him. I can only do it through Susana or Sofia. I think of him twenty-four hours a day, and I go to work less and less. Physically, I just don't have the strength, and psychologically I have only one person in my mind the whole time: Giovanni. I only see a few clients, although I am still earning quite a lot of money. I stick to my regulars. The idea of being unfaithful has never caused me any problems. In fact, I've always thought such a thing was impossible. I thought you could be faithful, even if you had sex with other people. The body can be shared in a way that the soul cannot. But ever since Giovanni, I've felt bad with any new client, though I can't explain why.

Today Pedro came to fetch me and spend the night with me. I went reluctantly, and even a little annoyed, because I knew I would have to put up with all his moaning yet again. I'm so fed up with it! I decided that in order not to be his mother once more, this time I would have to have sex with him. That would calm him down, and then maybe he would leave me alone. When he suggested taking me out to dinner I said no, why don't we got straight to the hotel. I could tell from the look in his eyes he was delighted with the idea. This was the first time I had taken the lead, and he could scarcely believe it. He didn't need asking twice. And what should have happened a long time ago happened now.

Afterwards, we were both naked on the bedspread, which on this occasion performed a very definite function: I used it to wipe away my floods of tears.

'Don't be like that, please. Nothing's happened, I swear to you,' Pedro murmured, trying to comfort me.

I had a knot in my throat that stopped me breathing and made the tears running down my cheeks even more painful.

'How would you know? You told me you've never taken the test.' I was sobbing as I tried to speak. 'You're a coward. Yes, that's what you are. I always get myself tested. Always, always, always!'

Pedro was horrified at seeing me like this, and tried to convince me there was no problem.

'Please, don't go on so. I've never done the test because there was no need. I've already told you, I haven't made love to my wife in four years. And apart from you, I haven't had any extramarital relations.'

'I'm not an extramarital relation!' I said in a fury.

Somehow, I had managed to start breathing properly again.

Then I saw the split condom in his hands and had

another panic attack. I got up and went and shut myself in the bathroom.

'Listen. Here's what we'll do. I'll go and have an HIV test tomorrow morning, and since I don't have it and you don't either, there'll be nothing to worry about, will there?'

His words bounced off the bathroom door. I could not reply; I was so angry with him for having deposited his semen inside me without my permission, for having been so useless at putting on the sheath, for wanting to give me too much love when I hadn't asked him for any in the first place. I hated him with all my heart, and was revolted by what had just happened.

I decided it was God's punishment. I got into the shower, determined to eliminate every last trace of my sin.

Out Of The Closet

30th October 1999

For the past week I've been feeling very bad about what happened with Pedro. And it's had an effect on my work. I've refused several clients I've been offered, and my spirits have hit rock-bottom. I've told Pedro I don't want to see him again until he gets the test results.

I am still getting on well with the other girls, and today I even confessed to Cindy what had happened. She looked very serious and tried to console me by saying there was very little chance that I could catch a disease like that from someone like Pedro. She also told me the same thing had happened to her twice, and that it was one of the risks of the job.

'You can never predict when there's going to be a dud condom,' she said. 'And the more often you have sex, the more risk you run.'

Curiously enough, that hadn't even crossed my mind until now, which made me even madder at myself. It can happen to anyone, but I blame Pedro for doing this to me, and Giovanni just for not being there.

Now Pedro has literally vanished off the face of the earth, which makes me fear the worst. I calculated that if I spent another night with him, even though I can't stand him, that would be the end of my AIDS paranoia. There's only one problem: Pedro has never been seen again.

As if that weren't enough, the brothel owners seem to suspect that I see Pedro outside the agency, and get him to pay me without giving them their half. It's not true! If they only knew.

Tonight I agreed to go to see a woman client. She turned out to be an upper-class girl of around twenty, who opened the door to me in a transparent white night-dress, with crochet work at the neck and sleeves. She was very pretty, but I was surprised to see someone so young.

The apartment looked immense, with high ceilings and an interior corridor that seemed to go on and on. She took me to a small reception room, and offered me a drink.

'I'm Beth,' she said, handing me the glass of whisky I had asked for.

'Are you on your own tonight?'

'Yes, my parents are away on a trip, and I was getting very bored, so I called up to get some company. Were you surprised at finding a woman here?'

'No, not at all,' I replied, as naturally as I could. 'What surprises me is to find such a young woman with such clear ideas. That's all!'

'I've often been told that. What can I say? I like men and women. Tonight I felt like being with a woman.

Besides, my boyfriend has left me, and I wanted to try to forget him.'

As we were sitting chatting, I heard a sudden noise in another room. We were not alone. I must have looked worried, because Beth immediately tried to reassure me.

'It's Paki, my dog. Don't worry!'

A lovely Alsatian came into the room, panting, with its tongue lolling out of its mouth.

'Hey there, beautiful! Come here, come here boy!'

The dog came over to me, sniffed at my legs, and then stuck its nose up under Beth's nightdress. She didn't seem to mind his intrusion, but started stroking his sides.

'This is my friend, right? We're friends,' she said to the dog, just in case it was thinking of jumping up at me and ripping part of my face off.

The fact that she had to say that to the dog did not reassure me in the least. On the contrary.

'Is he aggressive then?' I asked, joking. The truth was, I was scared stiff.

'No, don't worry. It's just that he doesn't like strangers. But he's a good boy,' Beth said, scratching his back.

There was something sensual about Beth that stirred me. She was as sweet as an adolescent, yet there was a sexual glint in her eye. As I was studying her more closely, I heard another noise from somewhere in the apartment.

'Beth, there's someone else here, isn't there?'

'No! Don't worry, something must have fallen. I'll go and take a look. You stay here!'

'Beth, please, it's all right. I'd prefer you to tell me the truth.'

She ignored me and left the room.

'I'll be right back,' she said over her shoulder.

I was convinced there was someone else in the apartment. And besides, Paki had not moved an inch. It must be somebody he knew, and Beth was lying to me.

Five minutes went by. I didn't dare move. Paki started sniffing me again, then yawned, and lay down at my feet.

'I can see you've made friends already,' Beth said, coming in and seeing the dog stretched out in front of me.

'Yes, more or less. I really like dogs, and I think he's realized that. So, what was it?'

'Nothing. The logs I have on the fire in my bedroom. Would you like to see it?'

This was a clear invitation to follow her to her bedroom, so off we went, glasses in one hand and handbags in the other, with the dog following on behind. The bedroom was large and very pretty. It had rustic furniture and a bed in the shape of a boat. The spotless white sheets were strewn all over it, while at the other side of the room was a hearth with a newly lit fire.

The bedside table was full of glasses with the remains of drinks in them, and with white stains on their sides.

'My boyfriend was here this afternoon. We were in bed together, and then we broke it off. Strange, wasn't it?' said Beth, sniffing a line of coke. 'Want some?'

She had scraped the remains of the white powder on the bedside table into a little heap. She wet her finger, dabbed it in the powder, and sucked it.

'No, thanks. I don't do drugs.'

I had a fleeting image of Beth flat on her back beneath a dark, muscular youth, and groaning as she came. They must have been taking coke all afternoon and then, when she was completely smashed, she probably told him to get out, tears in her eyes, to get out of her life for ever. And then later, when she recovered, she called the agency to send a girl so she could take her revenge on every man on earth, especially her boyfriend. I could understand that.

She put her arms round my neck and kissed me on my lips. Her tongue was hot and bitter because of the coke she had taken, and I soon began to feel my own tongue go numb. Despite this disagreeable sensation, we lay down together, until suddenly I heard another sound. I was sure this time it hadn't come from the fireplace. No, it was from a huge wardrobe standing next to the window. Alarmed, I struggled up, though Beth tried to keep me in her arms.

'It's nothing! Come back, you can't leave me all aroused like this!'

I didn't pay her any attention, but opened the wardrobe door.

'So it was a log in the fireplace, was it?' I shouted, catching sight of a shape hiding at the back of the closet. I reached in and pulled the man out.

'Hey you, come out of there! That's enough of playing hide-and-seek!'

I tugged so hard that he nearly fell on the floor. Then I saw who it was! I couldn't believe he would do something like that to me! Standing there before me was Pedro, as embarrassed at his failed ploy as at being discovered.

'What, it's you?' I shouted, for once forgetting my good manners. 'What the fuck are you doing here? Come on, explain yourself!'

Pedro tried to regain his composure, and sat down next to Beth, who seemed to be having an attack of hysterics. Her laughter filled the bedroom and set Paki off barking.

'I'm sorry, my love,' Pedro finally managed to say. 'I wanted to give you a special present, so I hired this woman to give you a good time. Afterwards I was going to follow you home and tell you the test results were negative.'

He lowered his chin to his chest, just like a kid who's been discovered being naughty.

'What kind of a present is this? And I bet you wanted to make it a threesome. I nearly died of fright when I saw you in there. And because you're incapable of getting a proper hard-on, you get someone else to do the work. And you hired a woman! You couldn't stand the thought of me doing it with another man, could you, you asshole!'

At least I'd got it all off my chest, even though I was already regretting half of what I had said.

'And who are you anyway?' I asked, turning to Beth, who had finally calmed down and was searching for any last grains of coke on the bedside table.

'Me?' she said, as if I could be speaking to anyone else. 'I'm the same as you. I do the same kind of work, but from home.'

She started laughing hysterically again. Pedro's efforts to calm her down came to nothing. I got my bag and left, slamming the door in the face of poor Paki, who had followed me out.

Pedro decided to follow me, and when he got out into the street he started to run to catch up the hundred metres' distance I was in front of him.

'Wait, Val, please wait!' he panted.

I waved to the first free taxi I could see coming down the street.

'Marry me, please! I'm begging you!'

'Go to hell!' I growled.

I went straight home.

Partner Swap

25th November 1999

Seven in the evening.

No sign whatsoever of Giovanni. He promised me he would come today and we could spend the night together. But Susana hadn't called to tell me I've got the night booked. I was on edge all day, and had the familiar sensation that for the second time in my life I was being betrayed. I tried to take a nap to relax, but I couldn't sleep a wink. In the end I went to the gym to work it off. I took my mobile, just in case there was a last-minute call. Deep down inside, I still hadn't lost the hope that I would see the Italian who had stolen my heart for a third time.

A quarter past nine at night.

I had been lifting weights for a hour, and was cursing all the men under the sun, when I got the call I had been waiting for all November.

'Remember, at eleven you're supposed to be at the Hilton Hotel.'

'What do you mean, remember? Susana, this is the first I've heard of it!'

'Well you know now, don't you?' she said, sounding confused. 'Mae and you are spending the night with those two Italians. You should be happy, sweetheart, it's all the more money for you.'

It was late, so I had to hurry. I flew home still dressed in my gym kit, and had a quick shower. The anger I had been feeling all day gave way to a sense of joy, so I did not even feel like taking Susana to task for not telling me earlier. Unfortunately I didn't have much time to get ready or choose a stunning dress, so I took the first I could lay my hands on, a black outfit I wore with a cashmere coat. I had to pick up Mae on the way, so I told the taxi-driver to wait. Mae looked divine, from which I concluded she had been told about the date much sooner than I had, because she had even found time to go to the hairdresser's.

Susana was waiting to give us a slip of paper with the hotel rooms on it. To my horror, I read:

Val and Alessandro, Room 624.
Mae and Giovanni, Room 620.

I couldn't believe it!

'I think there's been a mistake,' I blurted out to Susana.

'A mistake? Where?'

'With the names. You've got them mixed up. Surely they should be the other way round.'

Mae was looking at me defiantly, and said ironically, 'They must want a change. I was with Alessandro the last time. Now you can have him. I didn't like him anyway. I reckon the other one must be better in bed. I'll tell you tomorrow how the night went!'

I had to restrain myself from jumping on her and tearing her hair out. I could not believe it. How could anyone be so cruel: how could he lead me on to think he liked me? Not only that, but he was forcing me to go and spend the night with his friend! My head started to spin so fast I almost fainted. I didn't know whether it would be best to escape there and then, or to spend the night with Alessandro and be the best lover he had ever had, so that the next morning he could tell Giovanni what a fantastic night we had shared. I wanted to make Giovanni suffer, to die of jealousy.

In the end I decided to pluck up my courage, and we took a taxi to the hotel. We arrived ten minutes early, so I suggested to Mae that we had a drink in the bar. I needed something strong to be able to withstand the humiliation I was being put through. I still couldn't believe how shameless he had been. Would he dare look me in the eye? What if I never even saw him?

I asked for a straight whisky, with no ice. While I was drinking it, I could see that Mae was blissfully happy as she sipped her Fanta orange through a red straw. It seemed as though everyone was laughing at me, but I had no idea why all of a sudden I had become the clown.

We downed our drinks in record time, and left them on the bar. We hurried up to the sixth floor; I was still seething with rage. When we reached Room 620, Mae did her best to get rid of me at once.

'OK, this is where I'm going. Your room is a bit further down the corridor.'

With that, she knocked on the door. I stood rooted to the spot, determined to get a glimpse of Giovanni.

'I told you, your room is further down that way!' Mae said in exasperation.

It was Giovanni who opened the door. Alessandro was just behind him. They had got together in Room 620 and invited both of us in. Mae didn't like that idea at all, but she tried to conceal her anger and joked that maybe we could turn this into an orgy. My face was so long and sad that Giovanni noticed immediately.

'Is something wrong?'

'No, no, everything's fine . . .' I lied. 'Is it all right to smoke?'

'Of course. Smoke as much as you like. But let me take your coat.'

He came close to help me off with it. Mae sat on the bed and lit a cigarette, and Alessandro sat down next to her and started chatting. I did not feel like talking: all I wanted to do was to leave. I didn't have the faintest idea why I had come in the first place. After a few minutes I couldn't bear how proud of herself Mae looked, and my emotions boiled over.

'All right, let's get this sorted out. Since I'm spending the night with Alessandro, and Mae with Giovanni, I think we should be on our way,' I said, speaking directly to Alessandro, who was busy peering down the neckline of the woman who had become my very worst enemy.

Giovanni froze on the spot. Alessandro started to laugh, and soon Giovanni burst out laughing too, while Mae glared at me for being so rude. I felt like slapping all their faces.

'You're staying here with me, silly girl,' Giovanni said, when he had finished laughing.

'You're not going with Mae then?'

'With Mae? Alessandro's the one who wants to be with Mae! I chose you. What's all this about?' he asked, suddenly serious.

'I don't know, you tell me! I was told I was to spend the night in Room 624 with Alessandro.'

'*Ma no*, silly!' Giovanni said, slipping back into Italian.

He speaks good Spanish, but every so often he can't help putting in a word in his native language. It sounds so sexy!

'It's the other way round. They must have made a mistake!' he said.

What kind of a joke was this? I felt like crying for joy, but at the same time I was really embarrassed at the way I had behaved, so I asked if I could use the bathroom. I locked myself in for five minutes, until Giovanni came to find me.

'Are you feeling all right?' he asked in a worried voice.

'I am now. I'm a lot better. Is it true you didn't want to be with Mae?'

'Of course not! I promised I'd spend a whole night with you, and here I am.'

'You didn't want to be with her?'

It was plain he was really upset at what had happened, so his only reply was to take me in his arms. The other two had already slipped out, so we were alone at last.

'Not even for a second?'

We made love all night, and to my great surprise I found I could have one orgasm after another. Giovanni

307

didn't care who I was, or that he had paid to be with me, he didn't care about the time or what my true identity was, all he wanted to do was make me happy.

The next morning, after Giovanni ordered me a huge breakfast in his room, I finally gave him my phone number, making him swear not to tell anyone that I had done so.

But this was like signing my death warrant in the brothel. Even though I did not yet know it, my days there were numbered.

My Guardian Angel

In my descent into hell, I discovered a corner of paradise

When Giovanni and I met, I knew at once I would never belong to anyone else. It was as though he had put out the fire burning inside me all those years, and had given a final answer to all my questions about love, sex, fidelity, and one-night stands.

In my descent into hell, I had discovered a small corner of paradise. My very own God was a tall, mature man with dark hair going grey at the sides, a face the shape of a ripe pear, piercing green eyes, and strong hands with uneven fingernails. It wasn't that he bit them, but he chewed the cuticles around them. He had a couple of hairs protruding from his prominent nose. God even had a slight paunch, which delighted me. It gave him a vulnerable look, especially when I laid my head on it and started gently stroking him. I loved to poke my finger into his navel, even though he hated it. In the morning, God smelled of the breeze and of sliced almonds, of dew on roses, freshly chopped wood, of straw in a barn, of green grass after a storm. In the afternoon, his smell was of a newly published book, and wholemilk yoghurt, of a lion roaring at dusk. And of a soft, juicy peach without that dry taste on your teeth when you bite into one. God had a rebellious hair above his right eyebrow, which I always said hello to. Then one day it disappeared, and we both searched desperately for it in among the sheets. But the rebel hair had gone for ever. A month later, another one appeared. That was when I became convinced of immortality. God was constantly surprising me!

God had strange teeth. They were dazzlingly white, but crossed over each other. Whenever he laughed he looked like a little boy, still with his milk teeth. God never fought with me. When I got angry, he would stare at me with his huge, intense eyes, and give me little kisses on my forehead to help calm me down. God had the instinct mothers have when a baby cries. If I was frightened, he would take me in his arms and rock me in my invisible cradle.

God's mouth was thin, and a pastel-pink colour. It drove me wild when it said that he thought of me every split second of the day. God taught me to give the most beautiful present: kisses. He devoured my mouth. I was not so good at it, but he only rarely told me so.

God also spent whole nights crying, his head under the pillow and with Dvořák's *New World Symphony* playing on his stereo, when he knew I was with someone else. That was when I discovered for the first time that a man's tears are the very best gift a woman in love can receive.

God had one small defect: he could not pronounce the

letter 'c'. I tried to teach him, but we could spend night after night spitting without getting it right. God was really funny! But what I most loved about him was when he gave me his blessing. God was generous, and blessed me whenever I begged him to.

Odyssey in Odessa

8th December 1999

Ever since I gave him my phone number, Giovanni and I have kept in touch. At first he began to call me once a week, but soon we couldn't bear not to hear each other's voice every day. I am still working at the brothel, so if he rings and my phone is switched off, he knows why. So far he hasn't mentioned it, or objected in any way, but I know he doesn't like it. Once I thought I could hear him choking back his tears.

I haven't told him about my life, and he hasn't asked. Out of respect, I haven't asked him anything about his situation either.

Today Giovanni called to see if I could take a few days off in the middle of the month and go travelling with him. He has to sign a contract, and would like me to go too. It won't be easy finding an excuse to be away from the brothel several days on the run, especially since Mae has let slip to Susana that she thinks there's a lot of chemistry between the Italian and me. She suspects I've given him my phone number. She's jealous, and I wouldn't be surprised if she has told more untrue stories about me. The atmosphere is increasingly tense, and Manolo has begun to keep an eye on me in a very obvious way. Even when one of my regulars calls, he tries to get them to go with another girl, telling them I'm not there. He's trying to get them to wheedle information about me from the clients. I really don't think I've done anything wrong.

So I had to think up an excuse in order to be able to get away with Giovanni without problems. I decided to say I'd got a crippling bout of gastroenteritis.

12th December 1999

Odessa is a city on the Black Sea in the Ukraine. Giovanni and I have arrived accompanied by an official interpreter, a close friend of Giovanni's named Boris, and he has found us somewhere to stay in a dacha that was part of a Soviet-era resort.

It was a very cold afternoon. A seagull came to our window. I had never seen a gull at such close quarters. It sat on the verandah balcony outside studying us haughtily while we were making love against the chest of drawers inside. I was watching it too. From time to time I could see its greedy eyes fix on the toast Boris had prepared us, with a little caviar on the side. Yet it didn't move, as if out of respect for what it could see. I found myself trying to imagine how gulls make love, and whether they use their beaks in any foreplay ritual.

Giovanni asked me why I was so quiet, and if the bird was still there.

'It's watching us.'

Giovanni suddenly shouted, '*Porca putana! Fuori!*'

But the gull just sat there, like a kid's plump toy. I could just see it preserved for ever by a taxidermist on my bedside table. No! It would never fit. It was far too big. Giovanni was still thrusting inside me, groaning in his own inimitable way. Feeling him like that while the gull looked on gave me a strange feeling of entering another dimension. Everything was pleasure and nature. All at once, Giovanni slowed down: he couldn't concentrate properly.

Afterwards, he went for a shower. I took advantage of being on my own for a few moments to pick up his shirt and admire his initials embroidered on it. He has them on all his shirts. I liked to run my fingers over them and feel how the thread stood out. I passed my finger back and forth, imagining I was blind and reading Braille. This was a very special moment for me, and I didn't want Giovanni to come in and catch me at it. As soon as I heard he was about to finish in the bathroom, I put the shirt back where I'd found it.

14th December 1999

A black limousine with tinted windows drew up outside the dacha. Giovanni and I were sitting staring at the sea, realizing how it got its name. It was so dark it looked like a huge plastic bag. Only the murmur of waves on the shore reminded us it was made of water. The moon shone timidly far out on the sea, while bitter dark clouds clustered round on all sides.

The chauffeur got out of the limousine and opened the

passenger door. Giovanni and I held our breath. Then she got out. She was beautiful, in a black evening dress and wearing silver high-heeled shoes. Her hair was cut very short, with a small V-shape at the nape of her neck, which was so slender I could have closed my hand round it. Her shoulder bones were showing, which made her look like a fashion model, a treasure yet to be discovered. Her body was not yet fully formed: her breasts were like two drawing pins sticking through her dress, suggesting the rest beneath. She was truly breathtaking. Giovanni took her hand and led her to the house without a word. Inside sat Boris, filling his glass compulsively with vodka as if he was nervous before an exam. Giovanni wanted to offer him a present, and had invited this princess.

The princess of princesses sat at the table with Boris, and without asking his permission started to drink vodka from his glass. Giovanni and I looked on in amusement. I was fascinated by how young she seemed, and so I asked how old she was: I wanted to be sure she was above the age of consent. Boris translated for me.

'She says she's sixteen,' he said with a childish grin.

I nearly fell off my chair. Giovanni was almost as horrified. I felt as though I was an accomplice in a crime, responsible for something terrible that was about to happen. I couldn't bear the thought. I asked Giovanni to send her home, because I wouldn't allow anything to happen to her. I asked him, begged him on bended knee. Giovanni agreed, but said that perhaps she was fine with the situation. It was better for her to be with us, who would treat her well, than with some sadist who might subject her to anything. With or without us, she was

315

going to carry on doing the same thing. She even seemed to enjoy it. And when we asked if she would like to leave – we said we would pay her anyway – the princess decided to stay. I sat studying her, seeing myself reflected in this young girl. I watched how she moved, how she laughed. She was wearing a chain with tiny bells round her right ankle, which tinkled every time she moved and filled the entire room in the dacha with a strange, exotic sound.

She got up on the table to dance, and even though the music on the radio-cassette was noisy and horrible, she swayed languidly to her own rhythm. Boris was sitting staring at her from two metres away, glass in hand. Giovanni and I were watching the show from a battered old sofa, full of strange stains and cigarette burns that must have been left from previous nocturnal orgies. The princess, whose name was Yana, started slowly to take her dress off. I could feel myself blushing. It was her clear, innocent smile which made me feel awkward in these surroundings. But she appeared happy and at ease dancing this provocative dance for an audience of three. She leaned towards Boris and whispered something in his ear.

'What did she say?' I immediately wanted to know.

'She said you're very beautiful and she really likes your earrings,' said Boris, downing another glass of vodka.

This made me feel even worse. I put my head in my hands, as if this would help me vanish on the spot. When I felt I could look up again, Yana was sitting on Boris's lap, enticing him with the movement of her small round breasts in his face. All she had on was a fluorescent green tanga. Giovanni got up and switched all the lights out. Then the only thing I could see was the tiny V-shape bobbing up and down, until I felt giddy. I took my lover's hand and led him up the stairs to the bedroom. As we made love, I could hear Yana crying out down below.

The next morning I went downstairs very cautiously and found the princess completely naked, asleep on the sofa. I almost ran back upstairs as quietly as I could, and when I reached the bedroom out of breath, I looked anxiously for them. Where on earth were they? I finally found them on the floor under the bed next to my shoes. Making sure Giovanni was still fast asleep, I picked them up, went downstairs once more, and searched for Yana's bag. I didn't dare pick it up, but undid the zip and put my earrings into an inner pocket.

15th December 1999

The white enamel had chipped off the bath, and the shower handle was rusty. There was hardly any hot water, particularly at the times when Giovanni and I wanted to take a shower. We have no option but to grin and bear it. I grimaced as a jet of freezing water hit my skin. Giovanni thought it was a great joke, standing there watching me with his toothbrush in his mouth, the dazzling white foam just about to cover his pink lips. I rubbed myself all over quickly with the soap we had bought in Spain. (Ukrainian soap is a suspicious colour, smells awful, and is hard as a rock. So much so that when I first saw it I had said to Giovanni, 'Look, here's a pumice stone!') I jumped out of the shower still covered in soap, searching for the least disgusting bit of the floor to stand on to dry myself. Giovanni had to catch me to prevent me from sliding straight onto my backside on the cold tiles. We both ended up laughing out loud. So much for our luxury lifestyle.

Boris used the downstairs toilet, where there was only a washbasin, which suited him fine, he said. I was a bit disgusted at the thought, but couldn't blame him for not wanting to risk our arctic shower. In the bedrooms there were still traces of the old communist regime: microphones on all the walls, sensors on the windows. It seemed that microphones followed me wherever I went. The verandah was supposed to have a sea view, but the clunky concrete posts made it difficult to see anything. The outside balcony was where I left my running shoes, which by the end of the day smelt like a mongrel dog. Even Giovanni, who usually accepts anything from me, warned me, 'It's your running shoes or me.'

I did as he said, because even I realized they were unbearable.

Giovanni and I made love three or four times a day. I learnt how to do the crazy frog (sitting on the edge of the bed with my legs wide apart and masturbating myself while he looked on, occasionally pouring mineral water on my stomach), the French submarine (my small heart-shaped mouth aimed precisely, sliding down under the sheets until it screwed its lips onto his penis), and the *levretinha* (from the French word *levrette*, in other words doggy-style with an Italian twist). There was nothing Giovanni and I did not try in our lopsided bed. So far he has never shared me with anyone, but tomorrow there is to be an exception: she is called Kateryna.

Boris wanted to see the princess again, but like the good disciple he is, he wanted to share her with us. There was no way I was going to agree to the three of us making love with Yana, and Giovanni agreed. So Yana decided to bring a friend of hers, who was older and had experience in threesomes, according to the person we spoke to at the agency. That was how we came to meet Kateryna.

The two of them arrived in the same limousine that had brought Yana the first night. This time, our princess was dressed like an adolescent in a pair of short black shorts, a white tee shirt and platform heels worthy of a drag queen. The only protection she had from the cold was an enormous fur coat which she wore draped round her shoulders, and which looked incongruous with the rest of her outfit. I thought she must trust us a bit more this time, and had decided she didn't need to put on airs as a femme fatale. She seemed even more relaxed than before, and kissed us on both cheeks as if she had known us all our lives. We were all outside the dacha; I was sitting on the verandah facing the beach. She sat smiling at me, which I took as her way of thanking me for the earrings, which she was wearing. All of a sudden she turned round and called to her companion.

Kateryna was a very small woman with long curly blonde hair. She was wearing a blue dress with a pattern of tiny red flowers, and a wide blue leather belt that dug into what I suspected were more than ample hips. She had tremendous turquoise-coloured eyes, and a tiny nose that gave her a Japanese look. She seemed like a little puppy, too scared to smile much.

She shook my hand coldly, and I started to feel guilty again. Yana was trying to encourage her, and I looked over at Boris to find out what was being said. Yana was gabbling away, with Kateryna giving only a minimal response. It all sounded like Chinese to me, but I sensed that Kateryna wasn't happy about something.

When Yana took her hand and disappeared quickly with her inside the dacha, we all followed in single file into the living room, as if this tiny princess had suddenly become chief of our tribe. Yana looked all around her, obviously in search of something. Boris was completely hypnotized by her and seemed unaware of anything else. Kateryna looked embarrassed, as if she didn't know where to put herself, until I brought the bottle of vodka which I guessed was what Yana had been searching for. We seemed to have established some sort of understanding just by exchanging glances. Kateryna literally leapt on the bottle, and began drinking straight from it. The alcohol appeared to have an immediate effect on her, because almost at once she started to dance, with Yana muttering words of encouragement.

'What's she saying to her?' I asked Boris.

Boris jumped, as if he had been woken from a deep sleep. He listened, then told me, 'She's telling her, "I love you, you love me, that's all that matters. Remember that I love you, that we love each other, and everything will be fine."'

In the evening we filled the living room with candles, and Giovanni lit them one by one to create a more intimate atmosphere. It was perfect. In the candlelight Kateryna's dress became transparent, giving us tantalizing glimpses of her curvaceous body. Yana began to undo the buttons of Kateryna's dress, dancing slowly round her. As usual, Giovanni was sitting back on the ancient sofa, watching them closely and shooting a glance at me from time to time to see how I was reacting. I went over and sat next to him. He took me in his arms and kissed me on the forehead. Yana and Kateryna were entwined in a lengthy kiss: we could see their tongues hungrily seeking out each other's most sensitive parts. Giovanni and I did the same. He gently took off the woollen jersey I was wearing. I was lying back, fascinated by the deep lesbian kiss and by Giovanni's hands stroking me. Then I felt Kateryna's cold hands caressing my back and reaching for the clasp on my bra.

17th December 1999

I was unable to respond to Kateryna. Throughout our journey back to western Europe, I tried to explain to Giovanni why I felt so bad about what had happened in Odessa. When we went our separate ways at Frankfurt airport, I wouldn't accept the money he offered me for having gone with him. I didn't want to be paid. I left Giovanni with a look of bewilderment on his face and caught my plane to Barcelona.

As I rode in a taxi into the city, images from our stay by the Black Sea flashed through my mind: the seagull, the way we had laughed in the sordid bathroom, the black pebble beach that cut our feet, Yana the little princess, still a girl but already capable of giving a blow job much better than me. And the ridiculous, grotesque surroundings with all that communist concrete: how surrealist it had been! The lesbian dance that Yana and her friend Kateryna had put on the night before in the dacha, and then the moment when Kateryna had started to caress my back and take off my bra. I could see everything so clearly. And what was clearest of all to me was that I was madly in love with Giovanni.

Change Of Century, Change Of Skin

19th December 1999

I was quite anxious when I returned to the brothel. All the girls were there. To my surprise Isa, who was preparing her trip to spend Christmas in Ecuador, took me by the arm and told Susana we were going out for a minute to have a coffee. She wanted to talk to me.

'You know everybody's crazy, don't you? Men who pay to go to bed with women are crazy, but we women who agreed to go to bed with men for money are worse.'

'Yes, of course. But what are you getting at, Isa?'

'There are things the crazy girls in there have been saying about you, because they're jealous.'

'Like what?'

'Like that you're stealing all their clients, that you see them outside the apartment. For example that Pedro who comes every week, and who came back while you were ill, that Italian, and lots of others.'

'What's Pedro got to do with it?'

'Well he came and hooked up with Mae, and she's a

real snake. He said he was madly in love with you and you would have nothing to do with him. She turned it round and said you were seeing him outside. Mae's trying to get rid of you.'

These confidences seemed strange to me, especially coming from Isa.

'I knew this would happen one day.'

'Mae also says you've given the Italian your phone number.'

That was true, but Mae was only guessing, because she had no proof.

'Obviously she can say what she wants about me.'

'Yes, but Mae's been here longer than you have, and it's her Manolo will believe. You're going to have problems.'

I'd already seen that Manolo could be violent, and what I was most afraid of was that he would do me harm.

'There's also a rumour that you've got AIDS.'

'That's a lie!'

That really was too much. In his snivelling to Mae about his unrequited love for me, Pedro must have told her about the torn condom episode. And she had embroidered the story to suit her own ends.

'Who said that?'

'Who else but the same crazy blonde? She's trying to scare the clients so they don't choose you any more.'

I was thinking of a thousand insults to hurl at Mae, but I had to control myself or I could be in still worse trouble.

'If you tell them what I've just told you, they'll think I'm an informer, so please, don't say a word,' Isa begged me.

'Don't worry, and thanks for telling me everything!'

We went back up to the apartment. Mae, who was dressing up to go out with a man old enough to be her father, shot cynical glances at us from her mirror. I pretended not to notice. Then Manolo appeared, followed by Sofia, who was on duty overnight.

'Can I have a word with you?' Manolo said, looking as grim as if he had just committed a murder.

'Yes, of course,' I said, determined to deny whatever he said against me.

I could see Mae's face light up when she realized how angry Manolo was. She left with a final barb, 'There's going to be hell to pay,' as she closed the door.

'Is it true you see Pedro outside here?' Manolo asked me.

'No, it's not,' I said, speaking the truth. 'Who told you that?'

'The client himself.'

I was paralysed by shock.

'Well, he lied to you. He tried to arrange to meet me several times, but I always refused.'

'What about the Italian?'

'I've seen him three times altogether. That's all. Besides, he doesn't live in Spain, so I don't see how I could visit him outside the apartment.' This time I was surprised at how well I could lie.

'I've heard rumours that say different.'

'Mae must have invented them to do me down.'

'Why would she want to do that?'

'How should I know? Because she's jealous, I guess.'

'Just remember that here we don't like people trying to fool us. You're lucky, because I don't have any proof. But

I'm going to keep an eye on you, and if I have the slightest doubt, you're out on the fuckin' street, get it?'

He was already waving his arms about and threatening me. Sofia was watching from the kitchen doorway, gesticulating at me to tell me to stay quiet or things could get really serious.

I didn't feel I'd broken any rules of the agency, because I hadn't seen Pedro outside, and I hadn't charged Giovanni a cent. So I didn't in any way feel I'd taken something that wasn't mine.

In the end I said nothing to Manolo, because I wanted to go on working over the end-of-year holidays, although after the episode in the dacha in Odessa with little Yana, the whole business was beginning to revolt me.

31st December 1999

The end of the century seemed to have awakened everyone's libido, perhaps because of everything that had been said about it, that it would be the end of the world, that a war was bound to break out, that all the computers in the world were going to crash. People were afraid, and wanted to live their last hours fulfilling their wildest dreams.

Tonight we even had women coming in couples to live out those dreams. I was working all the time, with Cindy.

My mobile was switched off most of the night. When I put it on again I saw I had lots of messages, and started to listen to them.

Giovanni had tried several times to get in touch with

me. He had left messages on my voicemail wishing me a happy New Year. He had also sent a text message, which was the greatest surprise of all.

'It's wonderful to talk about love, but it's hard too. I think I love you . . .' He wrote the last words in English, because he doesn't know enough Spanish. That was the last thing I had been expecting.

The Rescue

I told Giovanni everything. What Mae had said about me, Manolo's suspicions and threats, my personal situation and the fact that I thought I was in love with him too.

'Get out of there at once,' he shouted down the phone, desperately worried.

'How am I supposed to do that? Besides, I've got my things there.'

'Forget your things, and jump on the first plane. They might know where you live and go and try to beat you up. You need to come and spend some time in Italy. And when you return, change apartments. All right?'

I thought he was exaggerating a bit, but I could tell from his voice how nervous he was, so I agreed to everything.

23rd January 2000

Last night I dreamed of Granny. She was running through a dense forest, pushing a pram with rusty wheels. It must have been autumn, because the ground was strewn with leaves of all colours. Granny had put her hair up in a complicated chignon, doubtless to be more comfortable. She was disguised in a long black coat with buttons all the way down it, like a military great-coat. She moved lightly and gracefully despite the thick piles of leaves under her feet. Then all at once she came to a halt, out of breath, and started to stroke the face of the baby in the pram.

Her caresses warmed my heart, and her sweet face comforted me. I felt as if she had always been there, that she had never been apart from me. She curled her fingers through the locks of my hair. I was overwhelmed by a sensation of infinite love, and when I turned to look up at her I could see her eyes were closed, but she was smiling because she knew I was looking at her. She seemed to be wearing pale pink lipstick, and her lips were moving all the time, as if she were trying to tell me something.

'Rest now, little one.'

To emphasize his words, Giovanni clasped me to him even more tightly. We fell asleep again in each other's arms, in this tiny hotel bedroom he has rented for me.

What Now?

Hassan called again. He is still trying to persuade me to go to Morocco to work with him. I refused. It doesn't interest me, partly because I want to be able to enjoy the slightly bitter chemical taste of Coca-Cola once again.

I haven't heard anything more from Felipe, but I know his business went bust. The idea of selling slices of life cannot have worked. No two ways about it: people are very boring.

Ever since she broke up with her violinist, Sonia has stayed single.

Angelika and I are still in contact. In fact, we've become great friends. However long we go without meeting up, it's always as if we had seen each other the day before. But I haven't heard a thing about Susana or Sofia.

I do know that the girls all left the brothel. Manolo was becoming unbearable, so they decided to move out. As far as I know, they are all still in the same line of work.

Carolina has broken off all contact with me, and I'm afraid she has probably fallen back into the arms of

Jaime – whom I've started legal proceedings against, with no results so far.

Pedro has left his wife and over time, we've become friends. We occasionally go out for a drink, just to have a chat.

Giovanni and I are no longer together. We stay in touch, though. I've tried several times to explain the process I'm going through, which is reflected in this diary. He supports me and says yes to everything I say, in order to make me feel good. Perhaps he thinks he's part of a very strange psychoanalysis. I know he does it with the best of intentions, and tells me I can always count on him. But it will never be the same.

I still have a very special relationship with my bathroom. It's the place where I can get rid of all that's still weighing on me psychologically, and sometimes physically too. Everything flows and gets flushed away; it's just a question of pulling the chain.

I don't feel sorry about anything. In fact, if I had to live it all again, I would probably do exactly the same. It may be hard to admit, and may seem strange to a lot of people, but the time I spent in the brothel gave me some of the happiest moments in my life, simply because it was there I met Giovanni, and there that I found the new woman I am today. I feel as though I'm changing my skin every day, like snakes do at different seasons. My skin now is much easier to bear – it's subtle, soft to the touch, and more impermeable to everything around me.

But I wouldn't want the reader of my diary to get me wrong. This book is not a *mea culpa*, nor the portrait of a victim of a harsh, unjust destiny. I am not trying to tell anyone anything. I wrote this for myself, and in that sense it's a completely selfish gesture.

Yes, I have been a promiscuous, insatiable woman. That was because I saw sex as a means to discover what everybody is looking for: recognition, pleasure, self-esteem, or, to put it more simply, love and affection. What's so pathological about that?

THE SEXUAL LIFE OF CATHERINE M.
By Catherine Millet

'One of the most explicit books about sex ever written by a woman'   Edmund White

The Sexual Life of Catherine M. is the autobiography of a well-known Parisian art critic who likes to spend nights in the singles clubs of Paris and in the Bois de Boulogne where she has sex with a succession of anonymous men. Unlike many contemporary women writers, there is no guilt in Millet's narrative, no chronicles of use and abuse: on the contrary, she has no regrets about a life of sexual activity. Catherine Millet's writing is a subtle reflection on the boundaries of art and life and she uses her insights on the role of the body in modern art to set the scene for her multiple sexual encounters.

A phenomenal bestseller in France and in all other countries in which it has been published, *The Sexual Life of Catherine M.* is very much a manifesto of our times – when the sexual equality of women is a reality and where love and sex have gone their own separate ways. Like *The Story of O*, it is a truly shocking book that captures a decisive moment in our sexual history.

'I thought it was the most honest book I had ever read on the subject of sex'   Rowan Pelling, *Daily Telegraph*

'A brilliant testimony of a life spent at the sexual front line'
Independent on Sunday

'Unabashed erotica . . . a straight-talking romp catalogued with savage wit by a Parisian intellectual'   *The Scotsman*

'Millet writes extremely well . . . it is neither pornography nor her coy younger sister, erotica, but a work of libertine philosophy'   *Times Literary Supplement*

0 552 77172 4

CORGI BOOKS

SUBMISSION
By Marthe Blau

You'll want to scream, but you'll be gagged.
You'll want to cry, but you'll be blindfolded.
You'll want to run away, but you'll be tied up.
You'll have no way of begging me. I'll do what I want with you.

A story of sexual obsession, domination and extreme desire, *Submission* tells of a young married Parisian lawyer swept up in a cycle of sado-masochistic lust. A handsome stranger she meets in the courts issues her with a series of instructions which she finds herself compelled to follow. As the violence of their encounters escalates, these acts will become a dangerous addiction that she can't break. But how far can she go and how much of her life will she risk in the process?

Based on the author's own story, *Submission* sent shockwaves through the French establishment.

'THE BOOK'S CANDOUR RIVALS THAT OF *LA VIE SEXUELLE DE CATHERINE M*'
Sunday Times

0 552 77237 2

CORGI BOOKS

3
A modern-day *Story of O*
Julie Hilden

Maya and Ilan have an unusual marriage: Maya agrees to tolerate Ilan's chronic infidelity as long as she can participate and he will never stray without her. To her surprise, she finds their threesomes as arousing as they are disturbing, and for a while, everything seems fine. But as Maya's writing career takes off and she becomes more independent, Ilan feels threatened, and opts for another kind of sexual experimentation – one that plays on Maya's fear and ultimately threatens her life.

A compelling chronicle of obsession and power, *3* brings new immediacy to a timeless question: What is the greatest sacrifice you would make for love?

'IN THIS TERRIFIC DEBUT, JULIE HILDEN DOES WHAT FEW WRITERS CAN OR DARE TO: SHE HAS WRITTEN AN EROTIC, TRULY SEXY THRILLER. *3* IS SMART, SEXY, STRANGE, AND IMPOSSIBLE TO PUT DOWN'
Dani Shapiro, author of *Family History*

0 552 77177 5

BLACK SWAN